Conceptual Modeling
of Complex Artifacts
—principles, past and modern models—

Klaus Wimmer and Nancy Wimmer

MCRE Publishing
www.mcreverlag.de

Acknowledgements

We thank buildingSMART International Ltd. for publishing and sharing information on openBIM, in particular the schema IFC4. We have amply used material copyrighted under:
© 2008-2017 of buildingSMART International Ltd.

Special thanks for their trust and support go to professors Friedo Ricken, Heinz Schelle and Dieter Schütt.

For their invaluable contributions, ideas and hard work we thank our colleagues Dr. Bernhard Bauer, Sabine Gandenberger, Angelika Hecht, Dr. Michael Kuchler and Bernhard Latocha.

We also thank all others engaged in our projects over the years who are too many to name.

We thank these experts on IFC and openBIM who helped us in many ways:

Karl-Heinz Häfele, KIT, advised us on issues of Part3 of the book and introduced to the European project STREAMER, which investigates advanced topics of modeling in the context of IFC.
Dr. Reinhard Wimmer provided us with sample models of functional systems and advised us.
The Karlsruher Institut für Technologie (KIT) provided the free model-viewer FZKViewer. It visualized most samples in Part 3.

Last but not least we thank the unknown creator of the Clinic-model.

7

Concepts matter

Concepts are prime tools of description. All industries, therefore, abound with concepts, and as new organizations, products and processes are devised, concepts keep mushrooming.

Nowadays, models describe buildings – the architectural form as well as the technical innards. Models describe what one needs to know during each phase of a building's lifecycle, from design and construction to operation and maintenance.

These models are built from domain concepts – the concepts used in the building industry. Never before, we assume, have the concepts of a large domain been designed with greater care, then formally specified and finally standardized. This laid the base for developing computer-aided design tools.

Our own approach to concept design dates back. We designed concepts to describe one company's products, communication networks. Soon, we arrived at the question: *What is a quality-concept?* And if many concepts must fit together in one model like the pieces of a puzzle: *How to design all concepts systematically?*

And we faced the question *How to conceive a complex artifact – an organization, network or building?* Should one view it as an object related to objects or as a system composed of systems or else? And what would the pros and cons be?

First, we will explain our approach, which started from scratch and went through trial and error. Then we will sketch approaches we consider state-of-art. This leads to questions worth pondering.

Therefore this book.

Table of content

Part 1

The System-concept

Part 1: The System Concept

1

Domain Concepts

Why you are interested in concepts, this I cannot make out, we were once told, *concepts are cheap. I can always invent a new one and give it a fancy name. My kids bring home new words and concepts every day.*

The researcher O. Andersen would probably have objected. After all he spent time and effort on one particular concept, *Boundary*, creating an ontology for it. *Boundary* happens to be a valuable concept in the field of computer aided design (CAD) since it expresses the shape and appearance of, say, a building via curves, solids and surfaces of many kinds. The boundary-ontology captures, defines and orders concepts like *algebraic curve, polynomial curve, NURBS curve, parametric plane, spline surface, vertex, edge, path, loop, wire shell* and more [Andersen (2007)]. They belong to the domain one could call *boundaries of physical objects*, have evolved in the course of decades, and are widely used by computers.

It pays to define *Boundary* precisely, even standardize it. Only then can computerized tools of differing makes exchange boundary-descriptions, share their meaning and cooperate.

Many domain-oriented concepts are built into tools for design and manufacturing (CAD / CAM). A tool for architects, for example, would know about a FireSuppressionTerminal and many other things to be built into a house.

Standards define vocabularies in an attempt to control the use of concepts. STEP, the STandard for the Exchange of Product model data, is an instance in case.

Since concepts abound in all sectors of industry – ranging from automotive to utilities – researchers are concerned about the multitude of concepts in use. Some call for conceptual rigor and envision formalisms to capture and define domain specific concepts. Later on we will introduce a modern approach of laying the conceptual base CA-tools can rely on.

Shape and form are key properties of a building and any of its parts – floors, rooms, spaces, devices etc. But there is more to a building, say, a hospital: the many subsystems dealing with water supply, heating, hygiene, waste, transportation and communication. Should one capture the concepts of all subsystems, too?

Domain concepts capture domain knowledge and are grounded on experience. The concepts *placement* and *representation* in the following example, have proven their worth in the BIM domain. BIM stands for Building Information Modeling and Part3 of the book will say more about it.

Figure 1 introduces the world of concepts using a popular notation showing that concepts usually are structured. The concept is named BIMSite and helps to describe a construction site.

The bit of XML-schema shown tells that a BIMSite has zero or several (0..*) buildings (BIMBldg), each of which has zero or several floors (BIMFloor).

We need not discuss the syntax now since we will deal with more such concepts later on. Suffice it to say that information is captured in form of XML-elements (marked by the letter *e* inside a square) and attributes (marked by the letter *a* inside a circle). Those interested in the underlying XML Schema 1.1 schema definition we refer to [Wamsley (2012)].

Part 1: The System Concept

Figure 1: Specification of the BIM-concept *Site*

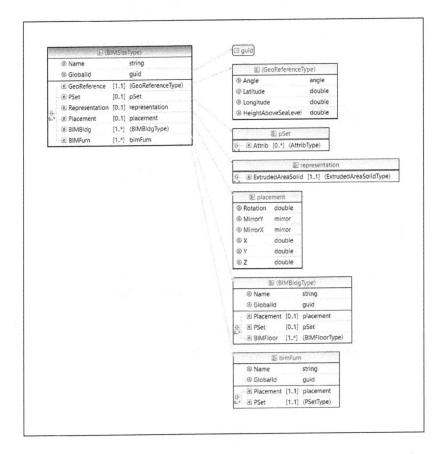

The schema of a BIMSite serves as a template when specifying a specific site, including buildings, floors and spaces. Figure 2 shows a specific concept named BIMSpace. It describes a space in a building according to the rules set by the schema. This instance of the schema has two main components named Placement and Representation. Representation describes the form which does not matter here.

Being a large domain, BIM abounds with concepts. Figure 3 lists a few sample concepts relating to function, risk and failure.

Obviously, there is no shortage of concepts. We can conceive things at will and often do. When it comes to concepts, we are living in a land of plenty.

15

Part 1: The System Concept

And yet, questions plague us about the concepts of this sample: Have we found practical and clear concepts – concepts one wants to deal with in more than one domain? Have we got too many of them or too few? Will the concepts fit together well when one builds a complex description of a technical artifact or an organization? Will concepts align like the bricks of a wall or will they overlap or leave holes?

Figure 2: Description of a space in a building

```
<BIMSpace GlobalId="..." Name="Basement 2" B="255" G="170", etc. >
<Placement Z="0.0000000" Y="4.6865500" X="17.9160000"
    MirrorY="False" Rotation="0"/>
<Representation>
    <ExtrudedAreaSolid Depth="2.4384">
    <CurveProfile Side="Outer">
    <Points>4.2406900,4.3817500;-4.2406900,0.8686470;-
            4.2406900; </Points>
    <Arcs>4,-0.4470640,0.0282540,1; </Arcs>
</CurveProfile>
</ExtrudedAreaSolid>
</Representation>
</BIMSpace>
```

Figure 3: Sample of concepts

- environmental condition, exposure, failure, fault
- function, functional concept, functional requirement
- functional safety, functional safety concept,
- functional safety requirement, hardware safety requirement
- harm, hazard, hazardous situation, intended use

Consider the concepts of Figure 3: *functional concept, functional requirement, functional safety, functional safety concept.* They seem to overlap in scope and, thus, share meaning. Should one revise them to avoid wasteful overlap and improve clarity? Should one know whether *functional safety* is a specific kind of *functional requirement*? This and more we would like to know. And how can we construct and define such concepts?

Need we dig down even deeper? How can we conceive a collection of concepts – or should we say *system of concepts*? Must it be a modular system – built of concepts which complement each other and aggregate well?

And which kinds of concept make complex descriptions easy to understand, use and maintain? Such issues are not altogether new. They mattered in the beginning of Artificial Intelligences: concepts were the tools to express knowledge and to reason with it.

No, we have not found the perfect answer to all of these questions. But we have thought about them, gained some insights and want to share them. Hence this book.

Concepts and models

In the 1980s, the complexity of two concepts amazed us: *Corporate Research* and *ISDN-Network*. The first referred to an organization, the other to a technical system. About 200 electronic handbooks and a database described the technical system, an ISDN communications network. Published in several languages, they would be used by network operators, the providers of communication services.

Then we were challenged to improve this technical documentation, i.e. decrease the effort of creation and increase its ease of use. At that time, Artificial Intelligence (AI) reached its heyday and so we considered putting all the facts stored in the handbooks into a knowledge base and use it in an expert system. It was to answer the questions of people who configured, operated, maintained and repaired this complex technical artifact. And if an error occurred, the expert system should recommend ways to fix it.

Corporate Research, in contrast, consisted of a few dozen distributed offices, each one dedicated to a specific subject of research. Twice a year they jointly determined the research budget.

In the 1980s, the world was gung-ho on office automation, supposedly the next multi-billion dollar market and AI, in particular, seemed the technology to build on. It promised to help solve the many routine problems popping up in offices and to automate office work, at least in part.

For instance, an artificial reasoner, an inference machine, should help with this small problem: The R&D budget had been already settled when one research department unexpectedly adopted a new project and thus had to revise its financial plan. Consequently, the overall budget needed revision, too. The current planning process had to be stopped, obsolete documents withdrawn and people informed. New information had to be generated and spread and the decision-making process resumed anew.

The challenge then was how to structure, describe and represent the planning process in such a way that a computer could make sense of it in order to perform routine parts of the process. It seemed the computer would have to deal with a myriad of concepts such as *plan, budget, process, right, duty, manager, task, project, report, schedule, cost, manpower, investment, risk, patent, resource* and very many more. And the computer had to know about all the projects envisioned, the departments pursuing them and the steps and rules of the planning procedure. To help control the planning process, the computer had to know what to do and what to avoid should the process not follow its normal course. Obviously, it had to know much more than the budgeting tables – the meager information stored in the planning database.

How to design such concepts? We guessed we had to avoid conceptual holes – not representable things – as well as conceptual overlap. Should the concept *task*, for instance, talk about a task's deliverables, the human resources, budget and schedule involved? Or should we design *task* and *schedule* as separate concepts? Perhaps we would find the answer while defining the concept *research-project* which somehow had to refer to the tasks involved, the budget and schedule among other things. In any case, the reasoning process would depend on it.

As we analyzed the planning process done at Corporate Research we became overwhelmed by the huge number of concepts implied. Yet even more concepts – many hundreds of them – were used to talk about ISDN networks, one of them being *Least Cost Routing* (LCR). Such technical concepts were listed in voluminous glossaries titled *Terms and Abbreviations*, which trailed all handbooks.

Part 1: The System Concept

The multitude of handbooks about the network was unwieldy though all of them could be stored on a CD, be nicely represented on screen and indexed in many ways. Experts got along fine, since they knew exactly which digital handbook to consult to resolve, say, this configuration issue: Would version 4 of the board LPG234 interface well with version 6 of the board IOR719? Experts knew of course what was meant by LPG234, what its function was and how it configured. They were happy using tables of content and string search to find what they needed. Not so the newcomers, and there were many of them around the world. They must have felt like an Internet user feels today, who searches for a keyword and receives 10.000 hits in return, not knowing whether a hit refers to hardware, software, a function, an interface, a problem, a solution, to old data or the most recent information.

We guessed, newcomers would be much better off if they could navigate through a model of the network. If this model visualized, say, a system's functional components, one could quickly locate the function LCR, then zoom into it to find the related hardware components, select the one of interest and study relevant features like its interface. Of course, models could visualize many other views of a system besides its functional breakdown. One could also highlight a network's configuration, hardware structure, software structure and other concepts which are easy to grasp.

How to design a model? Again we were confronted by the task of finding and defining the most important aspects and concepts pertaining to a network or any complex artefact. We tried to envision how a newcomer to network maintenance would browse a well-formed conceptual framework which organizes the network's many features systematically. But how to achieve it?

We were intrigued by the then-new idea of a virtual museum where visitors can virtually proceed from room to room, from collection to collection, from epoch to epoch, from topic to topic, from sample to sample, and see and scrutinize the objects of interest.

In the meantime, this idea has become reality, and what's more: interactive models abound today and can be inspected like a virtual museum. Architects create models of buildings and present them on screen or paper. Engineers, of course, have always visualized and worked with models of cars, chemical plants, etc. Other models are highly specialized like geographical maps, or expressed via mathematical and chemical formulae or via algorithms. So, some models are more visually appealing, understandable and navigable than others. Yet, they all present concepts.

Part 1: The System Concept

Some models serve as reference models: They prescribe how to talk about a certain domain and certain kinds of system. In the domain of construction one prefers to talk about a construction site which consists of buildings which in turn consist of floors and rooms, etc.

Other reference models prescribe how to present information, say, in the form of a handbook. In our case a reference model took the form of a document-type definition (DTD). Individual handbooks – expressed in the popular markup languages SGML and later XML – had to conform to the grammar of a DTD. A DTD would define for instance, that a handbook be composed of the three main parts ‹head›, ‹body› and ‹rear›. The head, usually, contains bibliographic information, the body a sequence of chapters – describing the topics of interest – and the rear term-definitions and indices. A chapter, in turn, is composed of one heading and one or more sections, holding paragraphs, tables and lists, images and links, headers, footers and more. DTDs cater primarily to form – to the layout and structure of text. This is why DTDs, which were indispensable to present information, were not our prime concern. We were concerned with content – how to conceptually capture the object or subject a document describes.

The structure of content matters. Consider the table of contents of a document about Company X which has three chapters: 1. Objectives, 2. Rights and Duties, 3. Assets and Debts. On first sight, this structure seems practical because it is understandable and seems to keep things apart which don't belong together. But when taking a closer look, the discrimination of rights and assets seems flawed, since rights may count as assets. Why then keep them apart?

Consider the case of a company acquiring a patent, thus gaining the right to use and market an invention and gaining an asset of value at the same time. Thus, following the patent acquisition, two chapters need an update: the one on rights and the one on assets. Much would be gained if the update was confined to one chapter only. Then the workload of authors and the chance of errors would decrease.

Obviously, one should become clear about the concepts one uses in a table of content (ToC). When documenting company X, one should be aware that the concepts *right* and *asset* overlap in their scopes of meaning.

When the ToCs of many handbooks seem to overflow with headings, trying to document a complex artifact's many points of view, then the choice of proper concepts matters.

A technical documentation – like the 200 handbooks on ISDN networks – is a complex object by itself. It draws our attention to its structure: is it well-formed? The concept *Structure*, by the way, deserves our attention because we use it all the time and structures take many forms: Buildings are composed of rooms, software of modules, contracts of paragraphs, projects of tasks, documents of chapters. Even the right of ownership is composed since it comprises the rights to use, to sell, to rent and to donate. Structure, however, often remains implicit. Thus, we say: *this tree has branches and leaves* instead of: *this tree is composed of branches and branches of leaves*. But what may pass for a tree may not pass for a system. Therefore, structures will abound in this book.

Back to the roots

When we faced the task of designing concepts – the building blocks for the description of networks and organizations – we did not know, whether anyone had tackled this task before and whether a design-technique existed already. We did know that the design of database-schemas was well advanced, but believed it would not contribute much to our job nor would Formal Concept Analysis, a mathematical theory applied to discover concepts in databases. We guessed such formalisms would not help to identify the characteristics of a given domain.

We also knew that our colleagues who designed object-oriented software struggled with the kind of problems we wanted to solve. They designed objects according to common sense, not according to design principles. One colleague told us: *I am drowning in a sea of objects. If I only knew how to reduce their number, how to distill the essential from the optional.*

Sometime later, we were in for a surprise: we found that for centuries philosophers had taken great care to precisely understand, define and use concepts. One contemporary paper dealt with the evolution of the concept *freedom* over the course of centuries.

During the Middle Ages, philosophers such as Thomas Aquinas considered concepts God-given. Concepts – if collected and aggregated into an ontology – had the power to reveal the divine order of the world to human beings. At that time, new and powerful concepts such as *act* and *potency* were added to the ontology. Some such concepts of old influenced us profoundly.

Philosophers gave us an inkling of what it meant to deal with concepts. They emphasized the significance of aspects, points of view. The person John, for instance, could be viewed as a father, husband, manager, taxpayer, etc. Abstract things like *freedom* could be seen from many different angles as well, from the perspectives of a citizen, a slave, or a state. Philosophers taught us that it matters to name the point of view one has taken. It matters to say: from now on we will discuss *John-the-father*. And it matters to carefully choose the points of view when discussing an object.

It was the philosopher Thomas Aquinas who directed us to the Aristotelian Categories, which we deem one of the great achievements of mankind some 2500 years ago. Thomas, by the way, revered Aristotle so much that in 1245 he travelled all the way from southern Italy to the University of Paris to study his archived scriptures. Aristotle's ten categories like *thing, quality, quantity and relation* sharpened our sense of aspects. Categories must be generic, i.e. widely applicable – not specific like *red* or *1-meter-tall*. And all categories must not overlap in meaning. Nothing must be both a quality and a quantity.

Aristotle helped us immensely. In fact, most of his categories are woven into the concepts we will present.

These ten categories inspired us:

Figure 4: Aristotelian categories

1. *Thing (substance)*
2. *Quality*
3. *Quantity*
4. *Relation*
5. *Posture (attitude)*
6. *Place*
7. *Time*
8. *Having (state)*
9. *Doing (action)*
10. *Being affected (passivity)*

We were inspired because these categories apply to all things in our domains of interest, to every component of a network, to all units of an organization. Each department or network node may have a state or perform an action, be affected, relate to others and be located in space and time. Thus these categories matter; they are indispensable.

Many things can be seen under many points of view – for instance as state – a static thing – or as an event – a dynamic thing. In other words: a system may be described both as a static and a dynamic system, say, the construction and the operation of a motor. But we should keep both descriptions separate.

The categories are independent and complementary, and therefore modular. When describing a system, we may start by describing its quality and later add its relations. Adding the point of view *relation* leaves the view *quality* untouched. To be sure: by acquiring a new relation, the system's quality may change. But the relation does not count as a quality.

All categorical points of view seem important and practical. *Quality* is a practical view since qualities (like *green* or *approved*) are hard to confuse with quantities (like *100 MB*), relations or actions. And most things have qualities of many kinds.

Little wonder, Aristotle's categories inspired us to look for more categories pertaining to the domains of organizations and technical systems. And we found a few. For instance, we distinguish things of a physical nature from things of a non-physical nature. Later on, we will explain this discrimination.

Note that the physical aspect of a thing is most practical while more specific aspects like *mechanical* or *chemical* are of lesser relevance since they apply less frequently – at least in our domains. After all, we have never witnessed the chemical nature of a network being documented. Hardware, in contrast, is well documented.

What's in a system?

Aristotle named the first category οὐσία (ousia) which translates as *thing* or *substance* or *essence*. We see it as something which exists by itself and from now on will call it *System*. Early on, we were aware that it was inevitable in our job to describe things of a certain complexity. Thus, the concept *System* roused our interest since systems scientists maintain that we can consider most anything a system: a galaxy as well as a biological cell, a human being, a machine, or a communications network.

Part 1: The System Concept

We searched for a prefabricated and preferably standardized system concept we could use, but found none. We found informal descriptions like the following:

- A system is a set of detailed methods, procedures and routines created to carry out a specific activity, perform a duty, or solve a problem.
- A system is an organized, purposeful structure that consists of interrelated and interdependent elements . These elements continually influence one another (directly or indirectly) to maintain their activity and the existence of the system, in order to achieve the goal of the system.
- All systems have (a) inputs, outputs and feedback mechanisms, (b) maintain an internal steady-state (called homeostasis) despite a changing external environment, (c) display properties that are different than the whole (called emergent properties) but are not possessed by any of the individual elements, and (d) have boundaries that are usually defined by the system observer.
- A system is a set of interacting or interdependent component parts forming a complex/intricate whole. Every system is delineated by its spatial and temporal boundaries, surrounded and influenced by its environment, described by its structure and purpose and expressed in its functioning.

Though it is not easy to distill a common core from these definitions, they mention relevant points of view. So, should we construct a system-concept, we better think of elements, structure, boundary, environment, etc. A most simple concept could look like this:

System
    Self   (description of the system itself)
    Environment   (description of the system's environment)

This concept contains a discrimination of views: *self* versus *environment*. They are complementary, i.e. categorical. Using this schema, one would first describe the system or thing itself, then its environment, which means the rest of the world. The schema is impractical, of course, because it is abstract, saying nothing about a system's self and environment. Besides, nobody would be

24

interested in the entire environment. Instead, one would want to know how the system relates to certain other systems populating the environment. Thus, a slightly better concept would look like this:

```
System
    self
            boundary
            structure
    environment-relations
```

This schema guides the author a little more in that the system itself is described in terms of its boundary and structure. And the broad concept environment has been replaced by the narrower concept of environment-relations, which helps to describe how the system relates to certain other systems. The schema is still a crude one and must be further refined. In particular the discrimination *boundary* versus *structure* is an odd one. What kind of structure is it? The system itself may have a structure like a car, assembled from parts. The boundary, however, may also have structure and in fact usually does. Surface is a kind of boundary. And the surface of a building is intricately composed of many parts, i.e. shapes and forms, as we will see.

```
System
    self
            boundary
                    boundary-structure
                    boundary-characteristic
            structure
    environment-relations
```

So, we better design a concept which gives a boundary a structure of its own, keeping it apart from all other types of structure. Later we will turn to this issue. The example clearly shows that it not only matters which views we choose, but also how we discriminate them and fit them together in a concept.

Part 1: The System Concept

With views of interest in mind we scrutinized collections of concepts being used in our domains. This included analyzing the concepts mentioned in the tables of content of technical handbooks. We also studied the glossary of terms used in a Handbook of Organizational Science [Grochla (1980)]. We looked at tax forms and balance sheets, because they are so broadly used – by most every citizen and company. Here we found a golden nugget: the discrimination of *assets* versus *liabilities*. This practical discrimination reminded us of a discrimination used some 700 years ago – *act* versus *potency* – or as one would say today: *active* versus *passive* things. Passive things, by the way, are not active, but may have the potential to become active.

2

Views and Discriminations

Some views, notably those implied by Aristotelian Categories, somehow seemed to be of greater value for constructing concepts than others, although initially we did not know why. We hoped they would serve us as the design principles we had been looking for.

Later we discovered that well-chosen discriminations would help us even further. They helped keeping things apart which should not become mixed up. They seemed to yield modular concepts, building blocks for complex descriptions. This notion pushed us on: we wanted to find out whether, how, and why modularization could work for us.

We found that it helps to ask for something and its complement. Answering this question helped understand the view taken. For example: Given the view *boundary* we had to know what is not a boundary. What complements a boundary? If boundary refers to the outside of a system, what is inside the boundary? We named the inside *body*. We could have also used the terms *black box* and *glass box*, because they mark precisely the distinction of *outside* versus *inside*. Similar questions ensue, for instance: What is a system if it is not static? A dynamic system perhaps?

Figure 5: Basic views and discriminations of a system

Self	versus	Environment-relation
Boundary	versus	Body
Characteristic	versus	Structure
Physical	versus	Logical, Institutional
Static	versus	Dynamic
Active	versus	Passive
Composition	versus	Order, Interaction

Step by step we came up with the discriminations listed above, arguing about the pros and cons of each one. We left out the famous discrimination of *time* versus *place*, as well as the discrimination *quality* versus *quantity*. They did not seem relevant enough to start with. We might use them later, if needed. The discriminations of Figure 5 seemed to fit, at least in the domains we were concerned with: networks and organizations. Did they indeed?

We had to answer many questions induced by discrimination: What is a system if it is not physical? True, before a communications network can operate, much hardware has to be installed in the field: copper lines, electronic boards, other physical things. But there is also a lot of software, which is definitely not physical.

While describing the planning done at Corporate Research, physical aspects did not matter at all, software mattered a little, but patents, contracts, objectives and resources mattered a lot. These things were neither hardware nor software, but what? Thus we felt we better have three types of systems: physical ones to describe hardware, another type to describe software and a third to describe the rest. And we decided on the discrimination *physical* versus *logical* versus *institutional* systems. Soon we will explain the meaning of these views.

And we had to ask ourselves: what is structure – is it merely composition – a whole and its parts? Or are there other kinds of structure? A structure, we believe, is defined by relations. But what types of relations are there? Take the relations of A and B: A contains B, A is taller than B, A moves B. Since these relations seemed of a different nature, we decided on the discrimination *composition* versus *order* versus *interaction*.

28

Finally we had to ask: what is not structure? Well, if *structure* talks about parts – how parts relate to each other and how they relate to the whole – we need a way to talk about the whole itself, be it a system, boundary or body. We could have named the discrimination *partial* versus *holistic* but did not, naming it instead *structure* versus *characteristic*. A characteristic characterizes an entire thing.

Some of the names for the discriminations in Figure 5 are unfamiliar, weakly defined and hardly self-explanatory – a major problem. No matter how we named the views and concepts they remained artificial constructs. Consider the System-schema of Figure 6, which we could use to model individual systems like Building-9 or Motor-47.

The schema names several views and related schemas like *body-structure* which in turn consist of sub-schemas to describe composition, order and interaction. Unfortunately, the schema introduces concocted names like *body-structure*. Unfortunately, too, many more such names will be needed, as we define more types of specific systems – systems which are static or dynamic, active or passive, physical or else.

Figure 6: System-schema-1

```
System
    Self
        Boundary
            Characteristic (a boundary-characteristic)
            Structure (a boundary-structure)
        Body
            Characteristic (a body-characteristic)
            Structure (a body-structure)
                Composition (a body-composition)
                Order (a body-order)
                Interaction (a body interaction)
    Environment-relations
```

We will refine the system schema, because systems can be viewed in various relevant ways. So we must answer questions like: what is a dynamic system and how does it differ from a static system? This means we must tell how static boundaries differ from dynamic ones. If we can't do this, we have failed. Refinement doesn't stop here, since one system can be both dynamic and physical. Thus, several views may combine and every combination leads to new concepts.

Eventually, numerous views and many more combinations of views need be explained. Seeing a system as a physical thing implies it has a physical boundary and a physical body. A physical boundary usually describes how the system extends in 3D space, the form of its surface, and characteristics like color. The physical body usually names the system's physical parts and tells us how they interact: one part may cool, support, or move another part or supply it with energy. But we better watch out: To express that one component informs or steers another, therefore we better choose a non-physical point of view – which we call the logical view.

It depends on the application, how many points of view one uses. The example in Figure 4 uses mainly the characteristics of a physical boundary, though with some precision. We will discuss this important view of a building later.

Depending on the application, we may leave open whether we describe static and dynamic aspects of a system. If we don't bother distinguishing the aspects *state* and *event*, we can throw static and dynamic things into one pot, e.g. how a car is constructed and how it performs – its size and acceleration. But if we choose the points of view well, we may start describing a component's states one after the other: first its hardware and later the software loaded into the hardware. Later still, we may add other dynamic aspects, describing a thing's lifecycle, performance, etc.

Needless to say that any system can have a name or ID. But it is not part of the system-description since names do not describe. For reasons of brevity we omit system-names which imply the distinction *name* versus *description*. Another distinction remains implicit: the description of a system itself versus its environment.

Getting acquainted with discrimination

It takes practice to become familiar with the views we have chosen. Thus the training course, which we had developed for the authors and editors of technical documentation, was well received. Here we choose an example from a domain everyone is familiar with: every-day life. Figure 7 mentions pieces of information about a person named *John* which we will turn into a description of John. In a first attempt to introduce conceptual structure, one may come up with a concept of John like in Figure 8.

Figure 7: Facts about John

1.	John	is 6 foot tall and grey-haired
2.	John	passed the MBA exam
3.	John	is group-leader
4.	John	weighs 80 kg
5.	John	can run 5 km
6.	John	lost weight during spring
7.	John	is watching the finals
8.	John	knows the tax law
9.	John	can analyze balance sheets
10.	John	learned new words during the Spanish-lesson
11.	John	decides the budget
12.	John	can supply customers
13.	John	earned a bonus during the project
14.	John	is negotiating a sales contract
15.	John	has the body-parts: head, torso, arms, legs ...
16.	John	has the expertise of: tax-law, Spanish-language ...
17.	John	has the rights to: buy, sell, hire, promote ...
18.	John	has duties: manage the department, make profit, ...
19.	John	belongs-to Sales-department-3
20.	John	reports to boss Bill
21.	John	is married to wife Sue
22.	John	is employed by A-Corp.
23.	John	is taller than son Bob

Figure 8: Draft concept of John

Self			
	Boundary		
		Physical view	Is 6 foot tall and grey-haired
		Logical view	passed MBA-exam
		Institut. view	Leads sales-team 3
	Body-characteris-tic		
		Physical view	Static-view • Weighs 80 kg • Can run 5 km Dynamic view • Lost weight during spring • Is watching the finals
		Logical view	Static view • Knows the tax law • Can analyze balance sheets Dynamic view • Learned new words during the lesson • Is computing today's expenditures
		Institut. view	Static view • Decides the budget • Can supply customers Dynamic view • Earned a bonus during the project • Is negotiating sales contract
	Body-structure		
		Physical view	Composition view Has the body-parts: • head, torso

				• arms, legs …
		Logical view		Composition view Has the expertise of: • tax-law, chess game • Spanish-language …
		Institut. view		Composition view Has the rights to: • buy, sell, • hire, promote … Has the duties to: • manage the department • make profit, …
Environment-relations				
	Composition			Belongs-to Sales-dept.-3
	Interaction			• Reports to boss Bill • Is married to wife Sue • Is employed by A-Corp.
	Order			Is taller than son Bob

By creating Figure 8, we have not put what we know about John into a passage of running text. Instead, we have used a schema to produce a concept of John. For example: we use views – if only crudely – to structure the concept. Views may come handy if we add information, e.g. that John is a member of a soccer team. We would put this new sliver of information under the view *environment-relations*. And if we were interested where John spends his time, we would check this view.

This selection of views may not suffice. After all, we still know precious little about John and may learn and store a lot more, for instance details about his career, projects, plans, resources, etc.

Early on, we generated a graphical presentation of a schema, calling it concept-box. The concept-box of John, Figure 9, was simply to generate and facilitate browsing the tiny domain of John. Clicking on the concept-box *A-Corp* displays its description. Clicking on the box Environment displays how John relates to the listed objects; that he reports to Bill and is married to Sue. When many objects populate the environment, which is the case with networks, we can group and categorize them, like the objects pertaining to John's professional life or to his private life. Or we may group all institutional things like company and boss and all physical things like house and car.

Figure 9: Simple concept -box

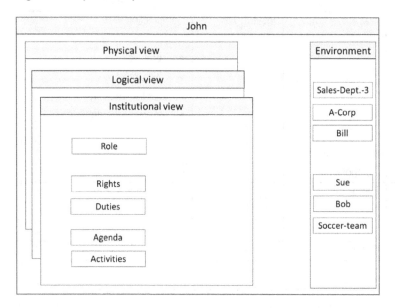

This simple example demonstrates that a conceptual structure can be visualized graphically. We could use markup languages like SGML or XML to represent concepts and present them, for instance, via HTML. Part 2 of the book shows that we used concept-boxes extensively.

Categorical discrimination

We benefit from categories and categorical discrimination mainly for two reasons:The discrimination of physical and non-physical things is categorical because the set of physical things does not intersect or overlap with the set of non-physical things. This categorical discrimination is practical since it splits the world of things precisely. And it is powerful because it distinguishes not only a handful but a myriad of things. It is more powerful than discriminating things which are red from those which are not. *Red* is a rare term at least in the domain of communication since there are few red things.

Red lamps warn if electronic boards are out of order. Otherwise, the domain of communication systems appears quite colorless. Thus, *color* is not a very practical point of view – compared, for instance, to the view *composition* which abounds.

All of Aristotle's categories are mutually exclusive. A quality is neither a quantity nor a thing, time, place, act or else. Discriminations are different: some combine and aggregate. A boundary – just like a system – can be static like the form of a ball or dynamic like the shape of an inflating balloon; a boundary can also be physical or logical or institutional. And it can be both static and physical. If it were static and physical, it could describe a system's physical extension. If it were dynamic and physical, it could describe a system's physical flows – the physical things a system exchanges with its environment via ports. John, for instance, has the physical ports *mouth* and *nose* to take in air and food. John's logical ports can take in information, his institutional ports accept tasks and duties.

It makes sense to combine the discrimination *boundary* versus *body* and the discrimination *static* versus *dynamic*. This combination yields refinements: a static boundary and body and a dynamic boundary and body. These refinements can be further refined using the discrimination *physical* versus *logical* versus *institutional*. By combining these three discriminations we gain a dozen specific concepts such as a physical dynamic boundary. They will be explained.

Many combinations of views look strange at first sight, but prove helpful in the end. This is the case when we combine the view *interaction* and the triplet of views *physical* – *logical* – *institutional*. Think of the interactions where someone kicks a ball (physical), promotes an employee (institutional) or informs a colleague (logical). This combination of views helps to denote what type of interaction takes place. And it helps to keep things apart which should not be mixed up.

Concepts – a matter of experience

Discriminations don't combine arbitrarily. Some combinations make sense, others do not. Suppose we introduced the discrimination *mechanical* versus *electrical*, which may make sense in some domains. These aspects will not combine well with the aspects *logical* or *institutional*. There is no logical system, say a software system, exhibiting mechanical properties. And an institutional system like a department cannot sport electrical properties. Thus we better not combine views at random.

Some constraints on combining views seem less obvious. Consider the view *interaction*. Should it combine with the view *boundary*? It would imply that boundaries were able to interact. But would *boundary-interaction* serve as a practical concept? We deem this concept impractical, because we believe boundaries neither interact nor cause anything. Only systems interact as well as their components which are systems, too. This is a matter of experience. Characteristics like color or velocity never cause anything either. Objects like blond hair or a speeding car may cause something, but not the properties *blond* and *speeding*. At least, we have not found any proof to the contrary.

We believe it makes sense to restrict interaction to the interaction of systems or body-components. We better prevent the interaction of boundaries. Characteristics do not interact either, nor do environment-relations. Computer-based tools can enforce such restrictions or at least detect their violation. If we created a knowledgebase of a communication network, as we once intended, a built-in watchdog checking on constraints and implausible concepts would come handy. It would help to keep the knowledge base free of nonsense like *speeding surface*. If, on the other hand, an author writes for a well-experienced audience, s/he may demand the freedom of expression and the freedom to entertain. In the descriptions we dealt with, however, there is no room for wit, irony or allusion. Flawless precision matters.

Inevitably, we must rely on experience and commonsense when creating concepts. We know from experience that structures of many forms play a major role with complex artifacts. So, we better support the description of structures. And commonsense leads us to keep the number of discriminations and schemas small. After all, users must learn their meaning and how to apply them which is a challenge. To understand the concept *Physical body*, for example, one must understand what *body* and *physical* mean, how a body differs from a boundary and how bodies can relate. This needs practice.

In Figure 5, we have highlighted a few basic views and discrimination. We called them *basic*, because they are quite universal, i.e. applicable in most any domain. There are, of course, more useful views and discriminations, as one would expect. None of them we deem to be basic, however, since they are too specific, i.e. useful and applicable only in specific contexts.

One context stands out, however, which we call *System-characteristic* or *Body-characteristic*. In ordinary jargon, characteristics would be called properties. And later on we will discriminate static and dynamic properties, physical, logical and other properties, following our basic discriminations. But these discriminations do not suffice, since the number of properties seems boundless. This is why we have experimented with generic discriminations, applying to properties only:

Figure 10: Possible discriminations of properties

- Qualitative versus quantitative
- Functional versus structural
- Intensive versus extensive
- Intrinsic versus extrinsic

The physical characteristics size and weight are of a quantitative nature, temperature and hardness are qualitative. Quantitative properties usually change and decrease, if a system-part is taken away, while qualitative properties remain unaffected. An intrinsic property, like hunger, is caused by the system itself, an extrinsic phenomenon, like attraction, by its environment. These discriminations were hardly popular in the network domain, except for the discrimination *functional* versus *structural*. Functional characteristics were used to describe performance, structural characteristics to refer to layers, tiers or levels of the system and to the many aspects of connectivity, disconnections, network redundancies, etc.

The discriminations of Figure 10 are examples in kind. They may help to order the large sets of properties of complex systems. Properties tend to abound in certain domains, as we will see. A myriad of products and functions introduces a myriad of properties.

The possibilities to discriminate seem boundless. Physical characteristics may well be mechanical, electrical, chemical, metallurgical, and so on. Innumerable combinations of views are the result. They are indispensable for the many niches of application, say for an architect designing the plumbing of a building in cold climate. But they must also be understood.

We found that examples help a lot to understand views and concepts, since they can relate to the wealth of knowledge people already possess. Informal descriptions involving examples often explain a topic better than a formal definition. Some colleagues tried to apply formal rigor using logical methods and inference machines to define concepts. Starting with the schemas of boundary and body, they intended to deduct physical, institutional, static and dynamic boundaries and bodies. But they did not succeed.

Ludwig Wittgenstein, the philosopher, would have called our approach to capture a domain in terms of system-concepts a *language game*. He considered language to be a tool, and speaking a language to be a game and a form of life:

> A language game is not predictable. It is not reasonable or unreasonable. It exists like our life.
>
> Logic, in contrast, deals with all possibilities. It does not determine what exists in the world or not. Logic exists prior to any experience that something is the way it is

Thus, Wittgenstein made us believe logic cannot help us to conceive a domain. We cannot deduce its important categories, views and discriminations. Discovering and determining them remains a matter of experience and the way we live.

Our colleagues were influenced by researchers who considered the construction of an ontology to be a logical exercise. They had to fail. They had not read Wittgenstein.

Filling in the details

One can specify John's physical boundary – his appearance – in many ways: simply via a photograph, or by listing the sizes of his hat, shoes, shirt and pants. One may laser-scan his figure and store the scanned data in a file. One may store John's appearance in form of computer-generated imagery, a CGI-file or show his appearance in a video. We cannot prescribe how to represent the details of a physical boundary for a given domain. Various standards apply in the BIM-domain as we will show. Here, we only say what is meant by *physical boundary* which can be grasped intuitively.

Other types of boundary are not as easy to come by. What is a logical boundary? A boundary in general describes how a system extends in some space, in physical 3D-space for instance, or in a logical space. Clearly, if *boundary* is to be a meaningful concept for a system, it must be meaningful for all types of system.

When we struggled with questions like: *what is a logical boundary* or *what is a logical space*, we found it helpful to play with words and looked for synonyms. Instead of using the term *space*, we could use the terms scope, area, range, region or field. And instead of using the term *logical*, we could use the terms *mental* or *intellectual*. So, John could have a scope of competence and an area of expertise. A database would have a scope of information. An encyclopedia extends according to its scope of topics; and astrophysics may lie inside or outside its scope. Again we cannot prescribe how to describe a logical boundary. In the case of John we may simply list the subjects he has studied and the languages he understands.

Thus several types of boundary exist and many more forms of presentation. The boundary of a city may be presented by an area highlighted on a map or by a line demarcating the city limits. Boundaries are often structured like the surface of a cube, which consists of six sides. The area of a country may be composed by the areas of its departments. Characteristics apply as well: functional characteristics, for instance, state the size in square-miles, structural characteristics state whether the boundary is contiguous or full of holes. Holes, like the spaces for windows, are typical for the outside of a building.

The boundaries of John may be of specific interest to physicians, teachers, lawyers, partners and competitors. Some will be interested in his area of influence within an organization or in the area where he can rightfully market a product. Systems, finally, may also transit in many ways, bounded by start and end and passing through many phases. Lives, lifecycles, careers and evolutions are examples in case. Such transitions count as boundaries, too. Not only states, events too, are bounded.

Thus, many types of boundary exist and we will inspect this concept more closely later on. Then we will turn to the concept *body* of which many types exist as well. And because all boundaries and bodies have structure, many types of structure exist. They help filling in the detail. They are essential.

From basic views to concepts

Concepts and schemas guide us when describing things. The system-schema, in particular, guides us to describe complex things. So far we have caught only a glimpse of this concept's construction: it consists primarily of the concepts *boundary* and *body* – a categorical distinction which in turn leads to concepts used to characterize and to structure a thing.

To arrive at a more specific boundary-concept it helps to think of specific systems, e.g. static and dynamic systems. They must be fundamentally different, thus having fundamentally different boundaries and bodies. Assume *surface* to be a static boundary, *flow* a dynamic boundary:

- Static boundary: (a surface)
- Dynamic boundary: (a flow)

Think also of the static system *John* who has size and shape and of the dynamic system *John* who breathes, computes and negotiates. A flow describes what crosses the surface of a system, i.e. goes in and out of this static boundary. Flows are dynamic in that something changes or happens. The things crossing the surface are either originated by the body or consumed by it. By breathing, John causes a flow of breath. Furthermore, a flow can be physical like the flow of breath or logical like the input and output of data or ideas. And it can be institutional like the gain and loss of assets.

When specifying *flow* we want to denote its direction (in or out) and throughput – i.e. the kind of flowing things and their quantity per time, say, dollars or bits per second. When one speaks of a factory's output of, say, a hundred cars per day, one speaks of a flow. Common sense and experience tell us that *direction, time* and flowing things play a role when we refer to *flow*. We consider *flow* a Basic Concept and a key ingredient of the system-concept. Note that in case we want to specify a flowing thing like a car, we would describe it as a system. If the flowing thing was breath, water or another kind of mass, we would not do that.

Nothing happens at a surface at any given point in time. Of course, boundaries may change in the course of time like a tire turning into a flat tire.

Some boundaries are considered static, describing shape, from, size and location in some space. Physically, a surface may be the sphere of a ball or the floor plan of a house. Note that John's skin is not a boundary – it is part of a physical body.

Let us consider two more types of boundary:

- Passive boundary: (a surface)
- Active boundary: (a port)

The distinction *active* versus *passive* is frequently made in many domains, although it is not verbally expressed. Balance sheets, for instance, juxtapose active assets and passive liabilities – in German called *Aktiva* and *Passiva*. This discrimination goes back to the middle ages when it was phrased *Act and Potency* and used to reason about God.

A flow actually happens. A port, in contrast, enables a flow to happen. Via John's ports of nose and mouth the flows of breath and food can happen. Both flow and port are considered active. They differ in that a port is static, a flow dynamic. The ports of a system are a prerequisite for change, while flows actually change.

Figure 11: Types of boundary

	Active view	Passive view
Static view	**Port**	**Surface**
Dynamic view	**Flow**	**Transition**

Surface and transition are of a passive nature. They simply extend – physically in 3D-space and in time. Transition in a physical sense may, for instance, define the phases of John's development from childhood to adolescence, etc. Transition in an institutional sense may define the phases of his career from the start as trainee to serving as market analyst, then as department head until retirement. Transition in a logical sense may define the steps of John's market analysis from start to completion. We may neglect much of the detail, but look through the magnifying glass on a certain episode when the adolescent John served as an analyst and came up with a novel analysis. We could decompose the thought-processes involved and describe them in as much detail as needed. Expert systems have shown how to log such chains of inference.

Below is a trivial description of John, which could, however, be refined. For instance, by further decomposing the *adolescence-of-John* and describing him at the age of 20 and 22 or by adding other views. Note, we added the fact that John is 55 years of age as a characteristic of his physical transition. The description of John's surface in space may be challenging, his transition in time simple. Here we kept John's surface as simple as possible.

Figure 12: Simple Boundary-views of John

```
John
physical view:
    transition
        characteristic: date-of-birth 1935; age 55 years
        composition:    childhood, adolescence, ...
    surface
        characteristic: (link to a photograph-file)
        structure:      (void)
```

In order to understand and use the term *boundary*, we better understand *port*, *flow*, *surface* and *transition*. Some of them will be detailed in Part 3 of the book.

3

Basic Concepts

Naming Basic Concepts

Often people asked us why we came up with the terms port, flow, surface and *transition* why we did not choose other terms. We answered that our choice of names was rather small and we had wished for more options. But the terms had to name all the views selected and be familiar – somehow.

Some people insisted: *why in the world did you call the boundary of a static but active system port? Do you rely on a tacit notion of system?*

Of course we have a notion like anybody else. But notions won't do for computers. This is why we tried to move from a vague notion to a precise scheme. That usually led us to the question: Could we do without the concept port? We probably could not, because as one student phrased it: a system without a port seems dead. Of course we could give the concept another name, *interface* for instance. But the concept would remain. And we asked our listeners: *would you consider a system-concept to be complete without* the concept *port or interface?* They usually replied: that would run counter to their intuition, commonsense and practical experience.

People asked us too whether *port, flow, surface* and *transition* covered the notion of boundary completely, whether boundaries of a different make could exist or at least be conceived. We were glad when they asked hard questions like this, because they touched on the core of the matter.

We answered that we had no proof and we believed that proofs were impossible. Proofs were logical constructs, but we did not deal with logic, we dealt with domains, reality, life, practice, experience and utility, also with change and evolution.

And we encouraged people: if you can come up with a better scheme, we will adopt it on the spot. Until then, we rely on our approach to create concepts as systematically as possible – by searching for the most important points of view, by combining them in a sensible manner and by using all the resulting concepts. So chances are, unforeseen boundaries won't catch us by surprise.

Unfortunately, our main descriptive tools – the Basic Concepts – are abstract, artificial and unfamiliar constructs. Often they even demand a new way of thinking. We had to teach Basic Concepts – this we knew. But how to teach them best: this we did not know. Because the concepts are new and strange at times, we try to name them in a way which stimulates an intuitive understanding. We hope that *port* and *flow* are fairly easy to grasp – as well as *state* and *event*.

State and *event* are popular concepts, though they often remain weakly defined. People prefer the common notion that something can be either a state or an event, but not both. This strict dichotomy applies in some modelling languages where events or actions lead from an initial state via intermediate states to an end state. An event causes the transition from one state to another.

We imply nothing of the kind. We can see a system be both a state and an event. In fact, we have viewed John as several states and events – as physical, logical and institutional states and events.

Conceiving Basic Concepts

So far, we have merely introduced system-views. Now we are going to define systems by showing what their respective boundaries and bodies are and how they differ. In due course we will generate a number of new concepts which we must introduce.

We begin by distinguishing two main types of event: *Process* and *Product*. Imagine the process happening at an assembly line where a car is being manufactured by the activities of workers and machines. And imagine the product, the finished car, which has not existed before, but eventually comes into existence as an output, deliverable or result of the production process. Since both the car and its making are complex, process and product will be seen as systems with structures and characteristics.

Figure 13: Generic types of Event

Active view	Passive view
Process	**Product**

We recall a participant of a modelling course telling us:

I had my problem with views, the active and passive views most of all, but now I am beginning to understand. A process is actively consuming resources and pushing things on, step by step, till it achieves a product. At this point in time the process stops and vanishes. But this event has happened. The birth of a product has happened too, but then the product may just sit there passively, doing nothing. Active versus passive works nicely for events. Now I am curious, whether it works for states, too. Active and passive seem like the two sides of one coin and we need them both.

We guess if we had not found the discrimination *active* versus *passive*, we had to invent it.

Figure 14: Specific types of Event

	Type of Process	Type of Product
Logical view	**Computation**	**Information**
Institutional view	**Act**	**Achievement**
Physical view	**Performance**	**Work**

We distinguish three diverse types of processes: Computation, Act and Performance which will deliver diverse types of result. When producing, say, a car, these three types of process may run in parallel, involving workers and robots to perform, engineers and computers to compute, lawyers and funds to act. These processes output Information (e.g. logs and test results), Achievement (e.g. licenses and certificates) and Work (e.g. vehicles one can touch).

We would welcome more self-explanatory names of events, of course, names which help to intuitively grasp the meaning. Though everyone has a notion of act or achievement, but no one would think of our notion: special kinds of system. As things are now, one has to learn the meaning of *Act*: an institutional process.

Computation has similar defects. It does not convey the many things it subsumes: thinking, reasoning, calculating, guessing, inventing, etc. The name logical view has its shortcomings, too: It makes some people think of logical formalisms, software and computers. When we changed the name to cognitive view or mental view, people thought of humans. But no discrimination man versus machine should be implied. So, no matter which name we chose, people needed to learn its meaning from scratch – via definitions and examples.

Some discriminations, like *Self versus Environment*, seem easy to grasp. Not so *Active versus Passive*. People often think that a passive thing is static and an active thing is dynamic. But what is dynamic?

The answer remains vague: things are dynamic if they make something happen or bring about change – either inside themselves or in their environments; static things stay as they are but can affect the environment. A red Ferrari may cause the desire to race it. It is a static thing when parked, but has the potential to become dynamic and change its location.

Such an informal explanation together with a few examples seemed to suffice. People understood or at least accepted the term dynamic. And they loved to know that some basic discriminations have been so important, they even entered the English grammar. It allows us to distinguish between ongoing processes (via the progressive form) and past events. The same kind of distinction can be made via process and product.

People also wanted to know why we need the dynamic view at all. Could the description of a car not contain the entire information? It could say that a car can move, change direction, play music, transport things and impress colleagues, and what its outstanding design would be. Would this not be all we need?

They were right to some degree. The many handbooks of a communications network did not describe processes at all, merely procedures. And many designs made by architects are void of processes. However we needed the dynamic view to describe the budget planning process at Corporate Research. Obviously, different applications require different sets of views. And people posed the fundamental question: *must we use all discriminations or can we neglect some of them? Which ones would be indispensable?*

After discussing the topic, people agreed, it would not be wise to dismiss all views since a handbook would end up as a flat list of many possible topics of description. So, we better choose some views with care to structure content. Figure 33 gives an example.

Figure 15: Generic types of State

	Active view	Passive view
Static view	**Operator**	**Operand**

The two main types of state we call *Operator* and *Operand*. Logical, physical and institutional instances of them abound in every household. There are devices like an oven and materials like the ingredients of a cake. The hardware of a computer (a device) comes with software (a method) to compute e.g. the data entered into a tax form (a concept). Bill (an agent) may insure something (an act) on behalf of his role, rights and duties (his authority).

The distinction is clear cut: Operators have the potential to do something, perform a process. Operands, in contrast, don't have this potential. Usually, they are acted upon by being input or output and by being transformed. Or they simply enable action. An electric drill can be seen both as an operator and operand. The operator-view would describe drilling power, energy consumption, drilling speeds, motion (turning left and right). The operand would describe the casing of steel and the parts important for use.

Figure 16: Types of State

	Type of Operator	Type of Operand
Logical view	**Method**	**Concept**
Institutional view	**Agent**	**Authority**
Physical view	**Device**	**Material**

All types of State and Event differ profoundly, thanks to the categories employed, which is what we wanted to achieve. Now we can describe anything in terms of a dozen main system-views. They are complementary modules of description and in principle of equal rank. In case we describe buildings, the material-view may dominate, of course.

Here is a list of the dozen system-views we have introduced. It often served us – not as a table of contents – but as a checklist for describing the many facets of technical and organizational systems.

Figure 17: Main views of a system

Static views	Dynamic views
1. Method-view 2. Agent-view 3. Device-view 4. Concept-view 5. Authority-view 6. Material-view	1. Computation-view 2. Act-view 3. Performance-view 4. Information-view 5. Achievement-view 6. Work-view

All system-views carry different names. But in order to differ in content, their boundaries and bodies must differ, too. This we are going to show for Process and Product, Operator and Operand, and in doing so, explain these concepts.

Boundaries and Bodies Define Systems

We have found categorical views, discovered discriminations, outlined a system concept and refined it a dozen times. Now we have arrived at the most basic concepts, the ontological core of our approach to description – twelve types of boundary and twelve types of body.

Figure 18: Generic kinds of Boundary

Type of system	Boundary
Operand	Surface
Operator	Port
Process	Flow
Product	Transition

Since all boundaries can be characterized and structured we should ask: "How are they characterized and structured?" However, we will not deal with individual characteristics and structures, since too many of them exist by far. Via the myriads of characteristics and structures our descriptive scheme spreads out.

It would be an illusion to prescribe or standardize the description of everything. Characteristics and structures must be open-ended, flexible, adaptive, domain-specific and even object-specific. A descriptive scheme derives its power, we believe, from the clever combination of formal rigor at the core and flexibility at the fringe. This has been achieved in the domain Building Information Modeling (BIM) which we will discuss in Part 3.

Consider the fictitious levels of decomposition in the domain of anatomy: arm, muscle, fiber, cell, cell-core, molecule, atom – saying that a muscle consists of fibers, a fiber of cells, etc. On every level of composition other views apply: physiological, biochemical or physical views. Components are of a very different nature than the whole, and components on different levels vary widely. On occasion, things of a certain type decompose into things of the same type: a software-system decomposes into software-components, a building into building-components, a surface into fractions of surface.

We have found few generic structures, i.e. structuring patterns which apply repeatedly. But we could not distill structuring principles applicable to all things of the network domain. Likewise we could not find characterizing principles, applicable to all things of the organization domain.

Figure 19: Kinds of Static-Boundary

	Boundary of Operator	Boundary of Operand
Logical view	**Port of Method**	**Scope of Concept**
Institutional view	**Port of Agent**	**Scope of Authority**
Physical view	**Port of Device**	**Surface of Material**

Most anybody has a notion of port, be it a harbor or airport where ships, aircraft, people and cargo come and leave, where import and export take place. Surfaces are easy to grasp, too – as long as they are physical surfaces. Ports and surfaces bound several kinds of static system. In practice, ports and surfaces become highly context-specific and are named accordingly. Figure 20 shows a few examples.

Though both *surface* and *scope* mean extension in some space, scope sounds less awkward in certain contexts. Think of the broad scope of an encyclopedia which describes people and inventions, geography and history, plants and beasts, the universe and more. Textbooks, in contrast have a more narrow scope, describing, for instance edible mushrooms or the media law. John's scope of concept, finally, extends into many dimensions including his mastery of foreign languages, his professional expertise, his skills as a golfer and soccer player. Likewise the scope of his authority extends. Think of the rights and duties of the president of a company.

Figure 20: Examples of Static-Boundary

Type of Boundary	Examples
Port of Method	• The data- and control-interfaces of a software program; • John's way of absorbing the news
Port of Agent	• A clerk's way of absorbing complaints • John's way of assigning tasks to his staff
Port of Device	• Keyboard and screen of a PC • John's nose, mouth and ears
Scope of Concept	• The contents of a handbook • John's knowledge of the tax-law
Scope of Authority	• Town hall's right to collect tax • John's responsibility for marketing
Surface of Material	• The topology of a building • John's figure

Figure 21: Kinds of Dynamic-Boundary

	Boundary of Process	Boundary of Product
Logical view	**Flow of Computation**	**Transition of Information**
Institutional view	**Flow of Act**	**Transition of Achievement**
Physical view	**Flow of Performance**	**Transition of Work**

Imagine the little company producing firewood in five steps (a transition): it receives stems of trees (a flow) on Monday, cuts them into blocks on Tuesday, chops the blocks into logs on Wednesday, bundles the logs on Thursday and delivers the bundles (a flow) on Friday. The performance of cutting, splitting and bundling transits from day to day until the work (the bundles) is done.

The final sales of the wooden goods (an achievement) requires a sequence of acts – the transition of making an offer, accepting an order and fulfilling the order. These steps are independent of time, but must follow the rules of trading.

Figure 22: Examples of Dynamic-Boundary

Type of Boundary	Examples
Flow of Computation	• Input of weather data, output of a weather forecast • John is arguing for a new project
Flow of Act	• Town hall cashes the tax payments • John accepts the terms of a new project
Flow of Performance	• The company is shipping fire-wood • John is eating
Transition of Information	• The newscast presented the polls county by county • John learned the news on politics, then sports
Transition of Achievement	• Offering, ordering and delivering bundles of fire-wood • John applied for and then accepted the job
Transition of Work	• The machine sawed, chopped and at last bundled wood • John got up, took a shower, then had breakfast

4

What's in a System

We have introduced the boundaries of twelve kinds of system, leaving the system-bodies to be defined. Thus, the naming game will continue. We refrain from choosing entirely artificial names like *B-LDS* to designate, say, the Body of a Logical and Dynamic System, whatever it may be.

What makes the body of a system? So far, we can post a few features. A body has characteristics and structure – parts which can interact and follow an order. Via its body a system decomposes into subsystems.

At this point, we remember Aristotle who named the first category *substance* or *essence*, something which can exist by itself. Boundaries do not exist by themselves. A shape requires something which extends and takes shape. Only in Wonderland can Alice spot the Cheshire cat's smile lingering in a tree – the cat being invisible. What we said about boundaries agrees with commonsense, we hope, that a system exchanges flows with its environment using various port to accommodate physical and non-physical flows. The boundaries *surface* and *transition*, by the way, relate to the Aristotelian categories *space* and *time* which we neglected so far.

We will further rely on common sense when dealing with bodies, assuming that systems owe their existence to bodies. This statement, we hope, Aristotle might have agreed to.

When we speak of *body*, we speak of many things – of force, change, energy and substance. Again, such terms are difficult to grasp, since they are abstract, carry numerous connotations and have a special meaning in our world of systems. Why these bodies? We chose them because they differ categorically and each body harmonizes with one of our boundaries, together making up a well-formed system. Last but not least, the choice is compatible with our experience. Here is an overview:

Figure 23: Systems, bodies and boundaries

	Body	Boundary
Operand	**Substance**	**Surface**
Operator	**Energy**	**Port**
process	**Force**	**Flow**
product	**Change**	**Transition**

Basic Concepts stem from commonsense reasoning. It may begin by observing how matter, a substance, extends and takes form. This may lead to the idea that not only matter but other substances extend and take form as well. Concerning processes: some force must be at work in order to start a process and keep it going. Force, in turn, requires energy and if force is at work, change takes place.

On first glance, force and energy tend to be associated with substance – muscle or battery. Looking closer, we detect many types of force and energy. Desire and motivation may force a person to act, the promises made in a contract, the will to earn a fortune or the commitment to do good.

Figure 24: Dynamic bodies: Force and Change

	Body of Process	Body of Product
Logical view	**Force of Computation**	**Change of Information**
Institut. view	**Force of Act**	**Change of Achievement**
Physical view	**Force of Performance**	**Change of Work**

Physical force powers performance, Logical force drives computation, Institutional force enforces action: John's will, intention, goal, desire or duty makes him act. His obligations may be fixed by job description, contract or law.

Some computations are data-driven: running until the last record is processed. Other computations are quality-driven: running until they yield results which are sufficiently precise or comprehensive. Force, thus, seems intrinsic to all processes and energy to all operators.

Figure 25: Examples of Force

Type of Force	Examples
Force of Computation	• Unprocessed data while computing the weather forecast • Inadequate search result needing better recall and precision
Force of Act	• A company's objective for reorganizing the sales department • John's obligation to declare his taxable gains and losses
Force of Performance	• The strength of a dog pulling a sledge

Yet, forces are often difficult to determine. One cannot see a physical force nor John's goal to create a tax report. Since he is determined to fill in every section of the tax form – his goal decomposes into sub goals. Forces seem at work all the time and knowing them lets us understand what changes and why.

Change can take place in many forms. A new piece of information may replace an old belief. A handshake may alter the ownership of a horse. And an accident may crash a car. In order to document change one may have to refer to diverse things like believes, ownership, form and function.

Change can be multifaceted: a new contract involves not only a new document, i.e. paper, print and signatures, but also new insights and ideas, and last not least new rights and duties, gains and losses. Change may alter the characteristics of a system or its structure and may affect boundary, body and environment relations.

Change can also be complex: consider an assembly line where a product starts out small, but through many steps of assemblage results in a car. This change has possibly many facets and a delicate structure.

Figure 26: Examples of Change

Type of Change	Examples
Change of Information	• A company issued its annual report; • John corrected believes about politics
Change of Achievement	• A company increased assets by selling a patent • By his new role, John gained some rights and lost others
Change of Work	• A company shipped a ton of fire wood • John changed dress and ate dinner

The bodies *energy* and *substance* seem awkwardly named, once again. Most people we trained conceived energy to be primarily physical – i.e. nuclear, solar, electrical, thermal. Would energy make sense if it was not physical? But in the end they agreed that force needs energy like a precondition. One man phrased it this way: *energy feeds force, force consumes energy. I need gas to drive. And I need money to move anything, assets and capital energize my company. And nothing goes without credit.* And right he was – almost.

Figure 27: Energy and Substance

	Body of Operator	Body of Operand
Logical view	**Energy of Method**	**Substance of Concept**
Institutional view	**Energy of Agent**	**Substance of Authority**
Physical view	**Energy of Device**	**Substance of Material**

Duties, obligations and assigned tasks energize agent John to act, e.g. to order something. And his right to dispose of assets enables him to order. Thus, we assume duties (active) and rights (passive) to be essentials of agents, their institutional energy and substance.

Figure 28: Examples of Energy

Type of Energy	Examples
Energy of Method	• A mathematical theory or a logical calculus • John's skills of arguing
Energy of Agent	• The duties of a civil servant • John's obligation to educate his kids
Energy of Device	• The electricity supplied by a car battery • John's physical condition to run a marathon

To determine the energy of a method and the substance of a concept is a delicate issue, seemingly counterintuitive. But it makes sense to conceive the substance of a concept to be, for instance, software code, mathematical formulae, logical statements or natural language expressions. Consequently, the energy of a method would be conceived as a mathematical theory, a logical calculus or a formalism usable to compute, evaluate or deduce. We consider a logical statement to be passive – a logical calculus active. If the calculus becomes dynamic by being executed, reasoning takes place. Thus, even *logical substance* and *logical energy* – two truly exotic concept-names – gain meaning. One student once told us:

> *Of course I will never use logical substance as a heading in my documents. I'll simply name the heading Software and then use Xref-links pointing to software-code and software-descriptions stored in our repository. That's all.*

Figure 29: Examples of Substance

Type of Substance	Examples
Substance of Concept	• Software code, mathematical formulae, logical statements, natural language expressions • John's knowledge
Substance of Authority	• The rights of town hall to administer a community • John's budget to do his job
Substance of Material	• The glass, steel and concrete built into a house • John's skin and bones

For a long time we were not sure how to name the static, passive and institutional body. Occasionally, we favored the terms *resource* or *value*. *Resource*, however, seemed too broad in scope since it subsumes physical facilities as well as knowhow. The concept *value*, in contrast, seemed too narrow in scope, since it lacks structure. *Right*, however, suits fine. It needs a boundary, the area within which it is valid, e.g. a department. Town hall has the right to rule within the town. Rights can also have structure: town hall's right to rule is composed of a myriad of rights concerning police, schools and more. And a right may be characterized – intensively by its legitimation, and extensively by its value. Last but not least, the passive *right* is matched by its active twin *duty*. Thus, the concepts *right* and *duty* seemed to be the perfect choice as static institutional bodies.

The system-concept recurs

Basic Concepts need to be refined as a domain or application requires. Section 3 of the book exemplifies the enormous effort involved and various methods of refinement.

When refining the system concept, the system concept can be reused. For instance to specify the flow of a production process one may describe input, output and throughput. In the context of a process, discrete objects may flow, products for instance. They can be conceived and modeled as systems.

When modeling *Change*, system concepts may apply as well – if we choose to describe change explicitly as one system before and another system after the change and the differences between them. Relations can express the differences, i.e. what has been added, removed or altered in a particular manner. System views help to express changes of form and function, configuration and organization of products and processes – physical, logical and institutional.

What's in a relation?

Aristotle judged the categories *thing* and *relation* of equal rank. Yet, compared to systems, relations may be of lesser significance since systems come with structures and, thus, relations.

A lecturer alerted us to sharpen our minds when dealing with relations. He made his point clear by using the word *good*. What is it? An adjective? And what does it mean? Has it to do with ethics, character, social action? No, *good* by itself has little meaning. It gains meaning in context of a relation: something is good if it is good for something else. Relations often remain hidden - in case of the adjective *good*, the noun *marriage* or the verb *has*. The marriage of John and Sue implies a relation between them as well as the fact that a tree has leafs as components.

The mayor of our home town is responsible for many projects, manages many clerks, and affects many citizens and businesses. By being responsible, he is related thousand fold. When a relationship plays an essential role, we better become explicit about it and better not disguise it as a system-characteristic. Imagine John being characterized as *good husband* instead of being related to his wife.

The lecturer cautioned us not to overlook relations since we easily fall into this trap: teacher and student, supplier and customer, director and owner are merely roles in a relation. They are not systems like John, since John may fulfill all of these roles and more: as father, tax payer, etc. Our programming colleagues have often created objects when they should have crated object-relations. Little wonder they complained about mushrooming objects.

Things relate to one another if they are composed or ordered or interacting. But how, precisely, does a relation relate things? Here, the mathematical definition *a relation is a set of n-tuples* helps little. Think of the example: Bill informs Bob enthusiastically about the Golden Goal of the Soccer World

Championship of 1996. A relation could name the persons, Bill and Bob, and tell their roles – the informer and the informed. It could also tell that a process of communication, takes place and identify it. This communication process, a system, may in turn specify the topic, place, time and form of communication. Thus, the basic schema *Relation* may look like this:

Figure 30: Basic views of a relation

Relation
       Relation-structure
            thing-1
            thing-2
       relation-characteristic

Relation-structure refers to the parts involved and Relation-characteristic to the entire relation. The example *John owns bank-account* in Figure 31 uses an enhanced schema. Assume for now, that it is one of John's environment-relations.

The choice of an interaction relation to express the relation between John and his account was motivated by the assumption that John interacts with it by withdrawing, depositing or closing the account. It identifies the relating things and their roles. And we added a bit of information how the account is owned. The relation, however, says little about ownership. Ownership, in our terms, is a right, which is the institutional body of the system named John. We will look into that.

Figure 31: Example Interaction-Relation

```
John owns bank-account
      type       Interaction-relation
      name       own
      relation-structure
            thing 1
                  type              person
                  ID                John B.
                  role              owner
            thing 2
                  type              account
                  ID                DE92 7876 8020 97030
                  role              owned thing
      relation-characteristic
                  owns-together-with-wife, owns- legally, ...
```

A relation can serve as a fast and simple way to express an important fact. The relation *John owns bank-account* expresses a fact without describing John, the bank-account or John's right of ownership. We have often used a relation as a shortcut – to sketch a description we might elaborate later on.

After a relation informs that two pipes connect, a computer could work out the geometrical detail and fitting of a seamless connection to enable a flow.

A relation, however, may remain implicit if it can be deduced and become explicit. If the body-height of John and son Mike is known, the relation of Figure 32 can be inferred. Or if factory F produces car C, they automatically interact, F playing the role of cause and C the role of effect.

Figure 32: Example Order-Relation

John compares to son
     type   Order-relation
     name   compare
     structure
          thing 1
               type   person
               ID   John B.
               role   the taller
          thing 2
               type   person
               ID   Mike B.
               role   the smaller
     characteristic
               body-height-difference = 2 inches

This relation represents a simple case in a straight forward manner. Yet an order relation may also express subtleties, for instance the similarity of things or their neighborhood or the way in which boundaries and bodies connect in space and time.

Apparently, relations carry redundant information, at least in a fullfledged model. Still, relations remain practical modeling tools.

Some interaction-relations appeared repeatedly in the domain of Corporate Research to express which party did accept, reject or alter a proposal and start, cancel or delay some process. But they were merely denoted by a field in a database schema.

We assumed that hundreds of kinds of interaction relation existed and we would discover more every day. Interaction seemed a challenge, much more than composition and order. Besides, interaction and function seemed like the two sides of one coin – yet too numerous and fleeting to master.

In an early attempt to organize the multitude of relations, we collected verbs – like *own, heat, supply, control* – which we expected to express via a relation. Later we built a taxonomy of relations, using views and discriminations to classify them. It made sense to keep relations between physical things apart from relations among institutional things. When at last we thought how the dozen boundaries and the dozen bodies would relate, we felt we found a way to classify and manage the very many relations.

One customer – apparently inspired by Influence Diagrams – became interested in relations to express causation and justification, because he entertained the idea of a network-of-causal-relations. Among other things, it should let him trace back the cause of communication network failures to flawed maintenance measures. He envisioned a network of relations like this:

Relation
- Relation-structure
    - Thing-1 (a network-component)
    - Thing-2 (a maintenance-process)
- Relation-characteristic
    - Cause of interaction (a error-message)
    - Effect of interaction (a change-of-network)

He intended to infer whether the effect of one interaction became the cause of another interaction. But unfortunately, methods and tools to realize this idea network wide were not in reach. The idea remained a challenge for the future.

The challenge of structure

What is structure? Wikipedia puts it this way:

> Structure is an arrangement and organization of interrelated elements in a material object or system, or the object or system so organized. Material structures include man-made objects such as machines and natural objects such as biological organisms, minerals and chemicals. Abstract structures include data structures in computer science and musical form. Types of structure include a hierarchy (a cascade of one-to-many relationships), a network featuring many-to-many links, or a lattice featuring connections between components that are neighbors in space ...

63

So, a list of relations or a set of parts will hardly suffice to describe structure. Part 3 of the book shows how elaborate structure becomes notably the spatial structure of buildings and the functional structure of mechanical devices.

These structures differ in nature. And they differ from the structure of communication networks where a myriad of constraints apply to define functioning network configurations. After all, networks evolve and all components come in versions and variants.

Often a single type of structure dominates the models of a given domain. It structures boundaries or bodies.

The Basic Concepts propose 24 categorical kinds of structure. This wealth of structure presents a chance since modeling structure means a challenge, as we will see. The proposed structures can be tackled one at a time and in the end complement each other.

But how to structure anything? How to structure this book? This is not obvious. A few structures achieved a breakthrough and have been widely used like the famous 7 layers of Open Systems Interconnection, the OSI-model. Structure captures domain knowledge which would be difficult to represent otherwise and helps to cope with complexity through clever decomposition.

One pioneering engineer even thought of modeling the justification of structure – the reason why something was broken down into certain layers, levels, sectors or functional units and why an abstract structure was thought to be complete, sufficient and practical. He used structural characteristics to denote this meta-level information.

Structures impose constraints which need checking. Will a building's systems for Heating, Ventilation and Air Conditioning collide in space? Or, will a project plan use the same machine-resource at the same time in different locations?

We believe in research on structure. One may find out what ontologically diverse structures have in common and how they differ. How can structures relate which run in parallel like spatial and functional structures? And how should interaction be expressed? And so on.

5

Design of Concepts

Basic Concepts provide many options to fill in descriptive detail. Whether one fills in a CGI-file or French language text to describe a person's appearance, depends on circumstance. Text may suffice while one attempts to clarify a topic's conceptual scope and structure. After the contents have been sketched, one moves beyond text, perhaps using notations computer can interpret. But how to become clear about conceptual content and structure in the first place? How to conceive, for instance, the statement: *John has $1000 on his bank account.* How to transform this piece of text into concepts?

When working on a modeling task like this, we follow a routine procedure:

- In a first step, we identify the main concepts of the statement – the nouns and verbs to be represented. The statement deals essentially with the concepts *John*, *ownership* and *bank account*. The term *John has*, by the way, is ambiguous. In this case we decide that *has* means *owns*. John is not having an asset like he is having a cold. But whether John owns an asset worth $1000 or an account is yet to be decided.

- In a second step, we conceive the nouns and verbs as systems or relations. John is a candidate system and so is the account. Both can be related, for instance by an interaction relation, but other ways of expression may exist.

- In a third step we draft the systems rather crudely by identifying the important views which apply. We have drafted the concept *John* in Figure 8 and may build on it, though it does not mention that John owns anything. But this can be fixed. Now we turn to *bank account* by considering all Basic Concepts one by one and checking whether their points of view concern the concept to be designed. In other words, we check whether and how we can conceive the thing-at-hand – the account – as a system.

Figure 33 lists all candidate system views like a checklist and highlights those views we deem relevant for the modeling task.

Figure 33: Candidate views of the Concept *bank account*

	System-view	Boundary-view	Body-view
physical	**Material-view**	Surface	
	Device-view	Not relevant	
	Performance-view	Not relevant	
	Work-view	Transition	Change
Logical	**Concept-view**	Scope	Substance
	Method-view	Port	Energy
	Computation-view	flow	Force
	Information-view	Transition	Change
institutional	**Authority-view**	Scope	Substance
	Agent-view	Port	Energy
	Act-view	Flow	Force
	Achievement-view	Transition	Change

Some physical aspects are irrelevant, because we do not care how the Cloud stores and processes account-data. Only one physical view matters. Figure 34 lists what we want to say about the account.

Figure 34: Draft-concept *bank-account-1*

		System-view	Boundary-view	Body-view
physical	1	**Material-view**	Location USA	
	2	**Device-view**	Not relevant	
	3	**Performance-view**	Not relevant	
	4	**Work-view**	Years 2001, 2002, 2003	Updates 1, 2, 3
Logical	5	**Concept-view**		[file *Account-SW*]
	6	**Method-view**	Withdraw, deposit, transfer, print statement, ...	[folder *API-account*]; conforms to SEPA standard
	7	**Computation-view**		Reliable operation
	8	**Information-view**	Save-point 1,2,3	Balance 1,2,3
institutional	9	**Authority-view**		Euro account, Dollar account; Value $1000
	10	**Agent-view**		Certified operation
	11	**Act-view**	Legal documents exchanged	Certified account, Customer contract signed
	12	**Achievement-view**	Installed 2001; Fiscal periods 1,2,3; contiguous periods	Gain1, loss2, gain3; Growth 3%; No overdraft

Figure 35: Comments on Figure 34

1   For legal reasons we state whether John's account resides inland or abroad. Surface is the place to state the account's location USA.

4   The account's physical life is broken down – i.e. composed of years. And the account has been physically altered several times on a storage medium by a composition of updates. The terms *year* and *update* will be defined eventually

5   Reference to a file in a repository

6   Via a SW interface john may withdraw, deposit, etc.; a reference is made to a SW folder; The contained code conforms to an industry standard

7   The account's implementation has been approved as reliable

8   The account's balance has been computed and communicated 3 times, when Safe-points were created.

9   The account is composed: it splits into sub-accounts for different currencies – one for Dollars and one for Euros. An account-characteristic names the account's value

10 The account conforms to regulations and fulfills legal duties

11 When installing the account, interaction between John and Bank occurred (via documents and signatures). At last, it was certified that the new account has a legal owner via an act: the signing of a contract.

12 During an uninterrupted sequence of fiscal periods, the account gained and lost assets. John achieved an overall growth of assets and never overdrew

The concept is an example to show that we are interested in numerous but not all views. A bank's IT manager might be interested in precisely those physical views we have neglected, e.g. processing speed and response time.

Apparently we neglected a few aspects, the account's environment relations for instance – after all it relates to some server in the Cloud which runs it and to some legal entity which owns it.

We did not associate the views *rights* and *duties* with an account, although we may deal with them eventually. If dividends have been booked to John's account, the duty to pay taxes may ensue. But it will be John's duty, not the account's duty. Or it will be the bank's duty if it acts on John's behalf.

Figure 36, finally, shows that the concept *Account* can be presented in a more user-friendly manner.

Still, the question remains: would the concept serve its purpose? Is its scope too broad or narrow, is it too generic or specific? Is it redundant or incomplete? This we cannot tell since we left the purpose undefined. But many options exist to adjust the concept.

Figure 36: Concept *bank-account-2*

Item	Value		
Location	USA		
Lifetime	year 2001, year 2002, year 2003		
Recordings	update1, update2, update3		
Account report	Average growth 3%, no overdraft		
Asset development	Fiscal-period1	Fiscal-period2	Fiscal-period3
	Gained-value1	Lost-value2	Gained-value3
Balance	$1000		
Sub-accounts	Euro account, Dollar account		
Functions	Withdraw, deposit, transfer, print statement, ...		
Interface	[see File *Account-AP*]		
Conformance	SEPA standard		
Validation	Val-date1	Val-date2	Val-date3
	Balance1	Balance2	Balance3
Security	Trusted operation		
SW documentation	[see File *Account-SW-design*]		

We have set out to model the statement *John has $1000 on his bank account.* The concepts, so far, tell us a bit about a person and an account while nothing has been said about ownership. So, we are not done yet.

Figure 37 defines a relation between John and the account – an object of John's environment. It lists a few facts but says little about ownership.

Figure 37: Concept *John owns bank-account*

Aspect			Value
Type	Interaction-rela-tion		
Name	Own		
Structure	Thing 1	Type	Person
		Identification	John B.
		Role	Owner
	Thing 2	Type	Account
		Identification	DE927876 8020
		Role	Owned thing
Characteristic		Nature of owner-ship	Shared with wife
		Period of owner-ship	3 years

Considerations of use

The relation of Figure 37 is simple and to the point. Yet, is it practical? If every bank-account has an owner, we may extend the concept bank-account by adding the characteristic *owner*. Here, John's identification could be filled in. This little addition renders the relations between owners and accounts dispensable. John's bank at least may have all the information it needs stored concisely in a database. Issues of information management, thus, influence modeling.

John's company has different interests. When paying salaries to employees' accounts it batches transactions per bank. In this case, relations between employees and owned bank-accounts help compile the batch. To this end, relations need not be as verbose as in Figure 37. Relating the IDs of John and his account (IBAN) suffices. More information about John's ownership would be welcome, however, if change occurred, if John donates, pledges, bequeaths or shares property.

Figures 38 and 39 indicate that more could be said about John's ownership – a right he has. *Ownership* is an intricate concept. How much of it is relevant? Must it be known whether John's ownership is the same as Sue's who shares the account? Does *owning an account* mean the same as *owning a dog*? And what about the duties which come with ownership?

Figure 38: Concept *John's ownership-of-bank-account*

Aspect		Value
Type	Right	Ownership
	Owned object	Account DE92...
Structure	Composition	Right-to-use, Right-to-share, Right-to-cancel
Characteristic	Validity of ownership	national
	Period of ownership	3 years
	Value-of-ownership	$ 1000
	Nature of ownership	shared
	Contract	[see file *Account Opening*]

Figure 39: Concept *John's rights*

Aspect		Value
Name	John B.	
Body-of-Authority (Right)	Composition	• Ownership-of-dog • Right-to-drive-car • Membership of soccer-club • Ownership-of-account DE92...

About modeling

This little example introduces to conceptual design by applying the system-schema and system-views in a flexible but guided manner. Views and discriminations, characteristics and structures, and environment-relations, offer a conceptual framework, to be refined as needed.

Following the system-paradigm, models can start small and grow. Starting with the simple concept of John in Figure 8, one would incorporate *Ownership of bank-account* into the authority-view of John and elaborate other views of John likewise. The concept *Account*, too, could be extended in several ways. A textbook says:

> *A bank account is a financial account maintained by a financial institution for a customer. A bank account can be a deposit account, a credit card account, or any other type of account offered by a financial institution, and represents the funds that a customer has entrusted to the financial institution and from which the customer can make withdrawals. Alternatively, accounts may be loan accounts in which case the customer owes money to the financial institution. Etc.*

So, we may distinguish various types of accounts and model the bank's respective rights and duties and show how they relate to a customer's rights and duties. Dynamic views can complement this piece of model – e.g. the physical and institutional activities to set up and open an account.

The system-concept paradigm helps design a concept piece by piece and make the pieces fit together in context. After all, concepts usually function in context, even gaining connotations from context. A relation makes sense in the context of systems.

An incident which happened in the 1970s, the pioneering days of Artificial Intelligence, explains this. Then, a computer program named Tale-Spin generated quirky stories [Shank 1981]:

> *... one day Joe Bear was hungry. He asked his friend Irving Bird where some honey was. Irving told him there was a beehive in the oak tree. Joe walked to the oak tree. He ate the beehive ...*

72

... one day dog Bo jumped overboard and, because gravity pulled it down, both Bo and gravity splashed into the lake. Bo swam ashore, but poor gravity drowned. Gravity could not swim ...

Tale-Spin probably knew only a few facts: that Bo, like many pets, can swim and jump, that some entity, named gravity, pulls everything down and that whatever cannot swim in water drowns. Probably it knew little about the contexts of bear and beehive and of Bo and gravity. Views and relations could have expressed that gravity, being a force not a system, could neither pull itself down nor drown.

Had Tale-Spin known better, gravity could have been saved. Only the charming twist of the story had been lost.

Part 2 of the book discusses a more comprehensive example – one of the key concepts of the communications domain: *Call*. All our partners understood its meaning only vaguely and, therefore, favored a Call model they could understand and use. After all, networks brimmed with call-related features and new call-features were required all the time. But how to model *Call*? In a first step we chose to model *Call* as a dynamic system, the method at hand.

Part 3 then shows what it means to fully formalize concepts, so computers can use them. And it reflects the state of the art of domain-oriented modeling.

Part 1: The System Concept

6

Methods and Tools

Most anything can be regarded as a system – this has been the credo of system-theorists for over a century. Yet, the collection of thread, needle and button may be too simple to be viewed as a system, a nation's society too complex.

Tools can help when a system description becomes complex. Unfortunately, the variety of systems is boundless. Would tools make sense to help describe chemical plants and companies, hardware and software alike?

Documentation tools

Some tools have been devised to cope with variety – generic Document Type Definitions (DTDs) for instance. A DTD is a grammar which defines the structure of a document, in our case the handbooks of a communication network.

Figure 40 shows a fraction of a DTD, which prescribes that a book starts with a cover-section followed by an administrative admin-section for bibliographic information and a body which consists of one chapter of level-1 (chap1) or one or more chapters of level-2 (chap2), optionally followed by a glossary and other lists. The elements *hotspot* and *targetlink* may occur anywhere in the book.

Figure 41 indicates that DTDs specify their elements in great detail. Here, the element chap1 is composed of some 30 elements, among them one title, paragraphs, tables and chapters of a lower level. The figure shows a fraction of the composition of elements in a tree-like manner. Using the DTD, an author can be sure to avoid formatting flaws. All chapters appear in the same elaborate layout.

Figure 40: Overview of a Document Type Definition

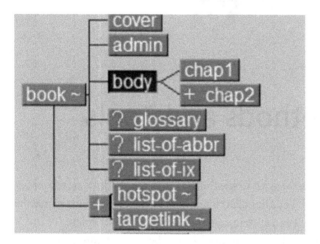

This traditional DTD served to generate documents expressed in the markup languages SGML. HTML and other formats were used to present documents to the reader. The DTD specified the form of presentation, not the structure of content. A table of content was generated from the headings of chapters before a document was prepared for publication.

The authors of handbooks valued the flexibility of their DTD-based editor which let them write about network features anyway they wanted and as many chapters as they wished.

Since the DTD applied to most any domain, it remained a practical but weak tool. Domain-specific proprietary DTDs existed, too, to document, for instance, airplanes or power plants, but dealt with content only on the side like our DTD which contained a tiny piece of content – a grammar to describe the domain's hundreds of maintenance-procedures. But the DTD did not help to describe anything else, although it could have helped to capture information on various components' dependencies on other components which was badly needed.

Figure 41: Document Type Definition (excerpt)

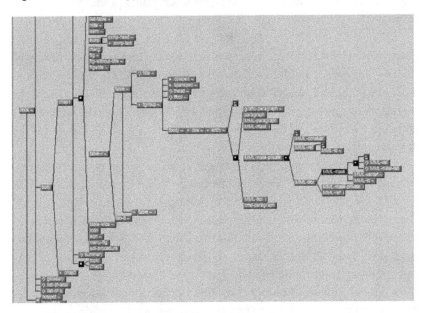

A different kind of DTD could do just that: help describe component-dependencies. Figure 41 sketches a tiny fraction of it. Eventually, a content-oriented DTD could do much more, we guessed: all Basic Concepts could be expressed in form of a DTD and, thus, be put to use.

Figure 42: Fraction of a content-oriented DTD

```
<!ELEMENT network-component (boundary, body, environment-relations)>
<!ATTLIST component id (ID #IMPLIED>
<!ELEMENT body (characteristics, structure)>
<!ELEMENT environment-relations,    (functional-dependencies,
                                    configuration-constraints, ... )>
<!ELEMENT configuration-constraints, (compatible-board-version, ...)>
```

Traditional DTDs resembled marvels of flexibility but in fact they were not. This we experienced when our company (A) began to cooperate with company B across the Atlantic. Because they intended to share products they had to share handbooks, too. However, both companies produced handbooks according to homegrown DTDs.

There was actually no need for two complex DTDs which served the same purpose. It is, however, a complex process to create handbooks involving teams of authors, translators, information specialists and a chain of tools. A DTD was at the heart of the documentation processes at A and B and to change a DTD meant to change processes and tools. Therefore both DTDs were kept in place. Consequently, handbooks conforming to the DTD of A had to be transformed to conform to the DTD of B.

This intricate conversion task taught us to care for the compatibility and modularity of DTDs and document structures. When the transformation was in place, we envisioned standardized definitions – expressed in XML – for all forms of text: for lists and tables, paragraphs and figures, chapters and headings, headers, footers, margins, etc. Having solved such issues of layout would give us the freedom to concentrate on issues of content: What must readers know to operate, maintain and repair a complex product?

This episode of exchanging technical handbooks between companies sheds light on a capital issue namely the exchange of information between the many diverse partners cooperating on an industry project. We will look into this.

Software engineering tools

The seminal Entity-Relationship-Model (ERM) was introduced in 1976. It employs a mere handful of views, notably *entity, relationship* and *attribute*. Any individually identifiable object qualifies as entity. But since *entity* remains undefined, anything qualifies as an entity, except a relation. A relationship can exist between entities, each of which can have attributes, like a name. Users are free to choose relations and attributes as they wish. Two special relations exist, however, the Is-a relation and the Is-part-of relation. The first expresses an abstraction as in the case: *John Is-a person.* The second models aggregation as in this case: *the football-team Is-part-of the football game and the football-stadium Is-part-of the football game.* This example aggregates a game (process), a team (agent) and a stadium (device). Obviously, aggregation did not model the composition of a system, but resulted in an arbitrary collection of things.

About twenty years later, a successor to ERM, the Unified Modeling Language (UML), was standardized and has become a prime tool for software engineering. An advanced version was published in 2015.

UML offers many forms of description to programmers, who are interested in key features of software like the flow of objects, flow of control, flow of information, and in a program's activity, action, interaction, input and output. Figure 43 presents an overview of UML diagrams of software systems, designed by Paulo Merson.

Figure 43: Overview of UML aspects and diagrams

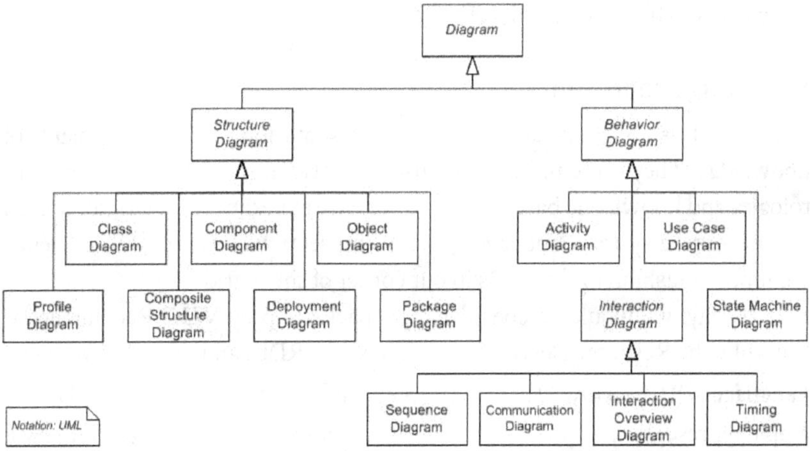

The names of the diagrams speak for themselves, and they are well documented on UML websites. Suffice it to add that UML employs several relationships, considered as logical connections of classes and objects, such as: Association, Inheritance, Realization / Implementation, Dependency, Aggregation and Composition.

A dependency is a basic relationship among objects. Example: a person can subscribe to – and thus relate to – any number of magazines. Predefined dependencies exist: one element (of software) may call, create, derive, instantiate, trace, use, etc. other elements. In our terms, such dependencies, correspond to interaction-relations among logical things.

An association represents a family of binary or ternary links. It is normally represented as a line. It can be named, and adorned with role names, ownership indicators, multiplicity, visibility and other properties. Via associations one can link any number of classes.

Most of the views the UML-diagrams mention seem compatible with our conceptual scheme and could be mapped onto the Basic Concepts under the static logical view.

Note the fundamental discrimination of *structure* versus *behavior* in Figure 43. It distinguishes the views *static* (structure) and *dynamic* (behavior), and subsumes the discrimination *passive* versus *active*. Since UTM deals with logical systems, several *Structures* correspond to the Basic Concept *Concept* and *Behaviors* corresponds to the Basic Concept *Method*. Thus we could use UML's formalisms to fill in the details of concepts and methods.

Knowledge representation tools

Another class of tools aims at the representation and management of knowledge. They serve to build and use semantic networks, taxonomies, ontologies and knowledge bases. Early on, we have experimented with tools used to build expert systems but gave up when this section of Artificial Intelligence went out of fashion in the 1980s in our corner of the world.

Today, we would re-consider tools backed up by W3C Recommendations like the Resource Description Framework (RDF) and the Web Ontology Language (OWL). How OWL works is exemplified at [OWL (2017)]. The example represents the concept Process, which implies the concepts *Participant, Precondition, Performance, Result, Parameter* and more.

The excerpt of Figure 44 conveys an impression of the OWL formalism. It says, among other things, that Input is a Parameter and its property *Parametertype* is restricted to non-negative integers of minimum cardinality 1.

We could express all Basic Concepts in OWL to lay the base for defining and expressing domain-specific concepts, e.g. the systems of a network, yielding a toolbox of domain-concepts to be used and shared. OWL offers interesting features. Its inheritance formalism helps to express concepts economically. OWL can also be the input format for reasoning engines. They are used in the BIM domain to validate complex models.

Figure 44: Example of the OWL formalism

```
<owl:Class rdf:about="#Parameter">
        <rdfs:subClassOf rdf:resource="&swrl;
        #Variable"/>
</owl:Class>

<owl:DatatypeProperty rdf:ID="parameterType">
        <rdfs:domain rdf:resource="#Parameter"/>
        <rdfs:range rdf:resource="&xsd;anyURI"/>
</owl:DatatypeProperty>

<owl:Class rdf:ID="Parameter">
    <rdfs:subClassOf>
            <owl:Restriction>
              <owl:onProperty rdf:resource=
              "#parameterType"/>
              <owl:minCardinality rdf:datatype=
              "&xsd;#nonNegativeInteger">1
              </owl:minCardinality>
              </owl:Restriction>
        </rdfs:subClassOf>
</owl:Class>

<owl:Class rdf:ID="Input">
                <rdfs:subClassOf rdf:resource=
                "#Parameter"/>
</owl:Class>

<owl:Class rdf:ID="Output">
                <rdfs:subClassOf rdf:resource=
                "#Parameter"/>
</owl:Class>
```

Building designers want to ensure, for instance, that their design adheres to various regulatory requirements. Therefore they convert models expressed in XML, the lingua franca of the industry, into OWL. And they use rules to define building constraints and restrictions. The reasoner then checks whether the model meets the constraints or not [STREAMER (2017), Deliverable D6.1].

Industrial tools

Tools support administrative and engineering tasks in many sectors of industry. They help manage human resources and customer relations, and they aid design, engineering and manufacturing tasks.

We dedicate Part 3 of the book to one such set of tools used in the domain of Building Information Modeling (BIM). Experts use them to design buildings – the architecture as well as the electrical and plumbing subsystems. Examples will demonstrate their capabilities.

Even readers not familiar with the BIM domain will be interested because these tools have absorbed an enormous amount of domain specific knowhow of materials, physics, space and structure.

Figure 45: Example model from the BIM domain

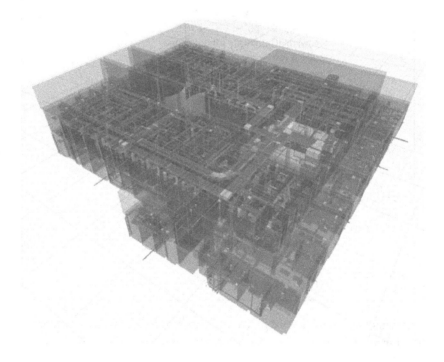

Standards [ISO 10303 (2017)] laid the base that CAD-tools can interoperate and designers and manufacturers cooperate in the field of BIM. We have studied this approach, being interested mainly in one question: which strategy is used to keep complexity at bay? A modern clinic, for instance tends to be very complex, integrating systems dedicated to ventilation, heating, cooling, water, waste, hygiene, energy, communication, information, transportation, security and more. Involved are many points of view, many structures, myriads of properties, dependencies and constraints. Thousands of concepts are needed to talk about them. Figure 45 indicates the multitude and variety of things in a building to be conceptualized. In Part 3 of the book we will examine this example.

How to capture all relevant objects aspects systematically? The openBIM-domain provides an advanced example. You may also dig deeper: the approach is well documented and accessible in the public domain at [bSI (2017)]. Amor analyses features of its evolution [Amor (2015)].

Note that some researchers have argued for the rigorous formalization of domain knowledge via ontologies and to lay this information open. An ontology of digital shapes, curves and surfaces was built early on [Andersen (2007)].

More recently, the research project Streamer [Streamer (2017)] investigated the future use of ontologies for the concepts of openBIM and related domains.

Part 1: The System Concept

Part 2

Past Models

Part 2: Past Models

7

How Ideas Evolved

We are going to look back to the beginnings, when modeling ideas emerged and were tested.

We could forego this exercise since decades have passed in the meantime. Yet we believe that background information helps explain why we did what we did. Ideas never came out of the blue, but responded to the needs, jobs and habits our colleagues shared with us. This happened in an industrial environment which shaped our approach to modeling.

Two causes triggered us to become engaged in modeling – as we have already explained. The first was the attempt to partially automate offices via knowledge-based tools which knew about an organization's processes and could perform part of them. The second was to provide better and cheaper information to those who maintained and optimized communication networks. And while we were working on these tasks we were influenced by the needs of developers, sales people and trainers – most of them engineers.

We felt, that in order to capture such information we had to model networks and organizations. We tried to stay up to date with the state of the art in modeling and experimented with several tools and methods: Petri-nets, the Structured Analysis and Design Technique (SADT), the Entity-Relationship-Model (ERM), Object Oriented Modelling (OOM) and, finally, the Universal

Modeling Language (UML). Our colleagues, in particular the software developers, preferred the Specification and Description Language (SDL), a state machine.

This chapter will display figures of a lesser image quality which we hope readers will excuse. Most figures depict slides, dating back many years. We use them unaltered because they bear witness of what happened. Some convey our way of thinking better than words could do, and even characterize our environment.

Figure 46: ERM – a seemingly simple method

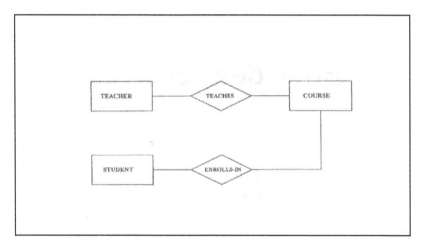

ERM examples appeared almost trivial, until a simple example left us stranded. The question was: How would we model a Person's Right to Drive a Car? Rights played a role as we modeled the planning process to determine a research budget. We began by jotting down entities and relations which came to mind:

Entities	Relations
Person Right Car Driving Process	? (driving process, person) ? (driving process, car) ? (driving process, right) ? (person, right) ? (person, car)

We liked our choice of entities, but on second thought were not sure why the choice was a good one and whether we could have done better. Things got worse when we tried to define relations. Of course we could invent arbitrary relations, name them and put them on paper as lines between boxes and diamonds. But was it worth anything? This we did not know, and worse, we guessed we would never know in advance, before we put a model to use.

While we kept on dabbling, we stumbled over a simple model of an oil-tank, which puzzled us (see Figure 47).

Figure 47: How to build a model?

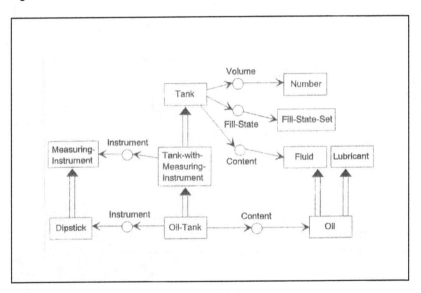

We could not make out why Content – apparently a property – was a fluid and Volume – another property – merely a number. And are the dipstick and the oil not both parts of the oil tank which just happen to play the roles of instrument and content? Should Dipstick relate to the Fill-state it measures? And why are Fluid and Lubricant look alike although they are different in kind? A fluid is a thing that could exist by itself while a lubricant cannot. It is a role oil can take if it is used to lubricate something else.

Our early attempts to modeling were discouraging. It seemed not only easy to create a flawed model – it seemed unavoidable.

How, then, could we possibly design big and demanding models like the model of a call? *Call* was a key concept in the communications domain. It's what networks are about: to connect persons or devices via calls, and let them exchange information until they hang up to end the call. Figure 48 mentions the concepts and aspects we planned to consider when modeling a call.

Figure 48: Ingredients of a complex concept

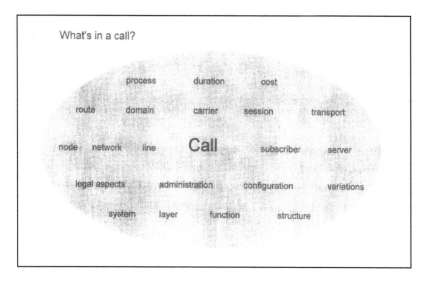

We soon noticed that *Call* was a rich concept and we would probably need months to model it if we had to. And we were uncertain how to go about. ERM, we felt, could not provide the guidance we lacked.

Sometime later, we did model the concept *Call*, including a sophisticated technical feature: *Call Data Recording* (CDR). Then, carriers were forced by law to record information on calls. But such recordings were suspected to intrude on people's privacy and, therefore, were heatedly discussed in public. Thus, our modeling endeavor challenged us in more than one way.

Figure 49: Challenging views

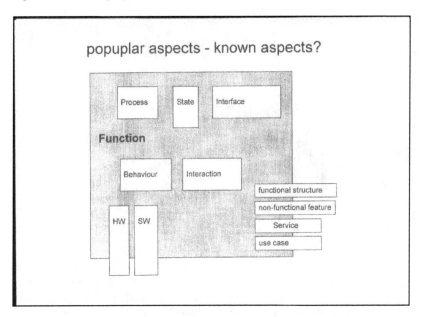

We began by putting a few aspects (see Figure 49) together which we deemed relevant to describe a call. We doubted whether it was a good selection since it dawned on us how very little we knew about these aspects. But we guessed, it would pay off if we made use of them.

We also guessed a thorough, multi-faceted and well-structured Call-description would pay off, if engineers, sales and service personnel, and managers could use it alike. A call model might even help customers to describe some complex requirements for their corporate networks.

Thus, in 1983 we entered the modeling arena –uncharted terrain, which intrigued us.

When we had to convince colleagues and managers that we were on course, we once let them work on a simple example, an episode of *Alice in Wonderland*: Alice meets the Cheshire cat with a black tail sitting in a tree and smiling at her. Later on, only the smile remains in the tree, but the cat disappeared. Discussing this ontological paradox deepened the insight on context.

Figure 50: A simple exercise

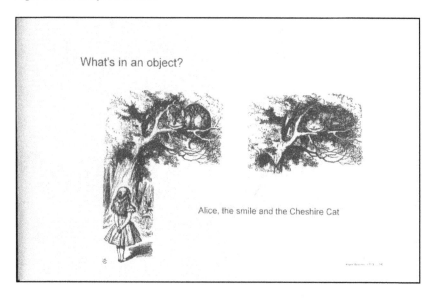

Our advice was a simple one, but it helped, in particular the last advice: *Put all things in context*:

> 1. Find independent things
> 2. Find dependent things
> 3. Classify all things
> 4. Put all things in context.

Simple models emerged, as in Figure 51. They built on entities and relations, integrated aspects and placed everything in context. Then even outsiders considered us to be on course. No one had a problem producing a simple, but expressive model.

Figure 51: introducing points of view

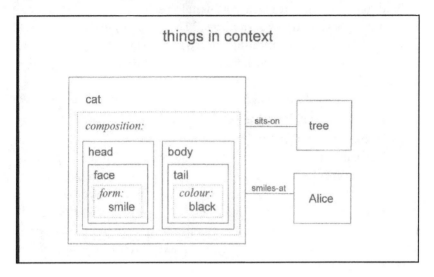

Managers felt it was a good beginning since the approach could be elaborated much further. They liked the approach because they knew about the complexity of technical specifications – requirements, designs, tenders and offers. Every one of them had eventually struggled with complex documentation before. All had built private models, sketching layers, functions, interfaces, dependencies, etc.

They appreciated context because they felt guided. A smile made sense only in the context of a face. And it was not part of the face, but its form. And a face made only sense if it belonged to a head which belonged to an animal.

A mere smile in the tree did not belong there. Via ERM it would be simple to express a smile in a tree and Alice in front of it. But something felt lacking: explicit context information.

Then the serious work began. We created dozens of models to learn about our shortcomings and we tested all tools we could lay our hands on, taxonomies being an example in case. Trying to lay a foundation we turned to philosophy, because we had heard that for centuries philosophers had cared for concepts.

Part 1 of the book describes what we found. We felt a breakthrough had happened when we discovered the virtues of discrimination principles. Finally we seemed to possess a handle on the myriad of system properties. And we realized some aspects were much more useful than others.

Then a phase of trial and error began. The taxonomy in Figure 52 documents one of the errors. It was an attempt to identify important concepts and put them in context. On first sight it did not look bad since all the things listed seemed highly significant.

Yet, attempts like this did not lead us anywhere and we remember well our discontent about it. Here, we had failed to explain and relate *Thing, System, Object, Function* in a sensible manner. And it was not obvious why we had failed.

Eventually, we gained the insight, that we had not failed on logical but on ontological grounds. It was a breakthrough when we learned that ontology matters. Therefore we were surprised about the ongoing ontology research. It was not at all concerned with distilling domain concepts, but with representing concepts once they were found. We recall a conference on Ontological Engineering at Stanford University where, we believe, ontology became confused with logic. So, we were on our own.

Figure 52: A trial gone wrong

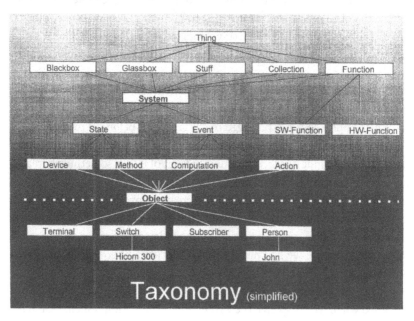

94

Figure 53: Initial views and discriminations

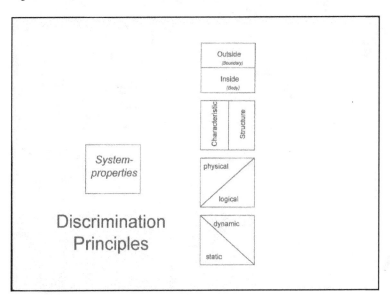

Our errors taught us to rely on the categories, views and discriminations we had. No other basis to build on was in sight. Starting from a few discriminations (Figure 53) we developed the system concept which we visualized as in Figure 54. Note the absence of the discrimination *active versus passive* since we were still underway to define the Basic Concepts.

This visualization should convey important features of our approach, for instance context. And it should highlight that very many aspects integrated nicely and were not at all chosen at random. Every aspect had found its proper place in a comprehensive descriptive scheme. And the visualization should bring home the idea that we arrived at a descriptive scheme made up of modules.

We admit that a few colleagues who used SDL felt overwhelmed by this schema. Compared to the simple schemes they were familiar with, our scheme looked outlandish.

Figure 54: Attempts to visualize the system schema

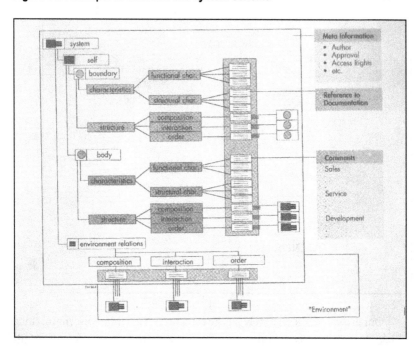

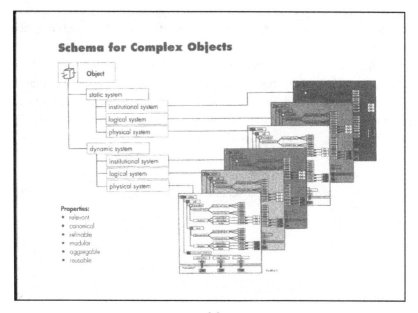

8

Towards Macromodels

Time had come to once more consider the applicability of our scheme. Had product models come within reach – generic models generated once and refined often and to be used for many purposes?

Figure 55 sketches the early assumption that a product model was the core of information underlying many documents. We assumed that service handbooks and operations manuals referred to a product. Therefore, if a generic product model was available, not only could it be re-used and refined in many ways and it would help to structure and elaborate documents in a compatible manner.

This overarching vision was of no practical use – given the means available to us. Yet, it inspired us to test our scheme: Would it accommodate the various kinds of product information generated by engineers for their own work as well as the product information generated for customers?

So, we mapped existing models used by product engineers onto our scheme, checking whether the aspects we found translate onto the aspects we used.

Figure 55: Refinements of a generic model

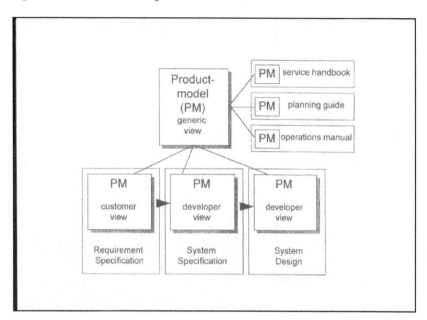

Figure 56 shows that we analyzed all aspects of the existing models developers had created. It had been easy to identify the aspects of interest, which we have highlighted. We will not explain them – they are too specific. Suffice it to say our scheme was rich enough to cover all aspects of all models considered. However we had no possibility at hand to incorporate the entire content of all models into one comprehensive model which we termed macromodel. That would require tools.

Part 2: Past Models

Figure 56: Attempts to map existing models

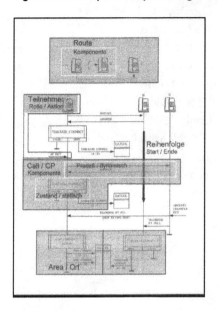

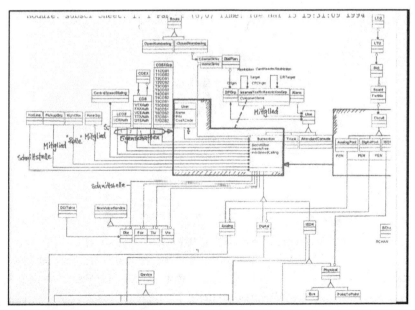

We realized the enormous task of building a generic product model – a macromodel – for many kinds of use. Therefore we followed a two-pronged approach: A macromodel should provide a generic, multi-faceted product description. And it should provide links into databases, repositories of development tools, handbooks, etc. – i.e. to very specific information. We guessed we should not integrate the mass of detail information into one model. We should separate the essentials from what our clients would deem trivial. In particular, we would not provide the level of detail, only developers had to know.

Still, we needed tools to create and check, visualize and use our models. Figure 57 sketches an early attempt to stitch several partial models together to display a comprehensive model. Simple HTML-based tools sufficed to link a few dozen parts of a model one could at least browse.

Figure 57: Composing a model from parts

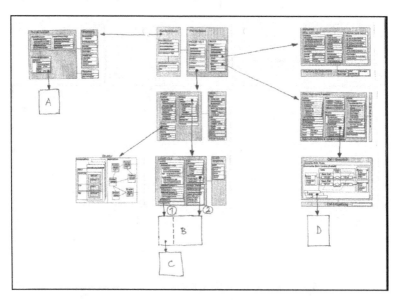

If a model was represented via SGML one could generate many forms of presentations like HTML. Such software tools we had built. Naturally, we thought of more powerful tools. So did the world around us. Visions of things coming up and catchwords spread as depicted in Figure 58.

Figure 58: a vision of the future

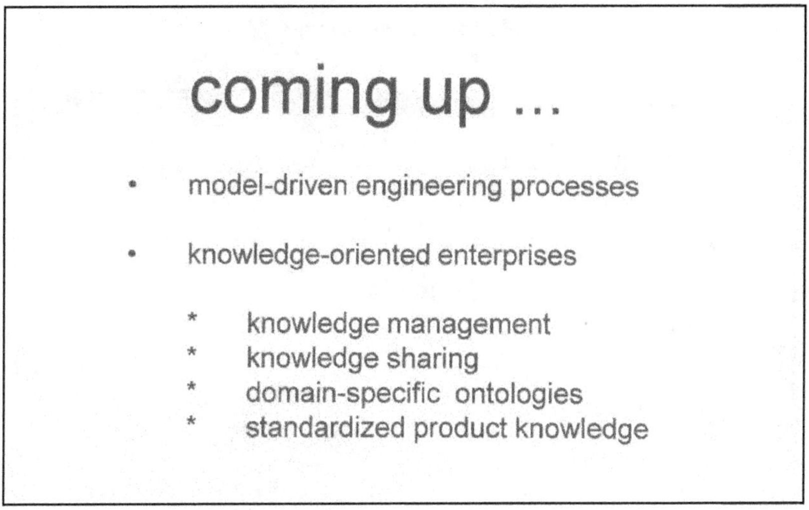

coming up ...

* model-driven engineering processes

* knowledge-oriented enterprises

    * knowledge management
    * knowledge sharing
    * domain-specific ontologies
    * standardized product knowledge

Still we hesitated to join the visionary bandwagon. After all, we had just witnessed the demise of the expert system movement and seen the hype of Artificial Intelligence falter.

Still we carried on experimenting. Figure 59 shows an attempt in the early days of network management when developers and customers alike struggled with the challenges involved. It highlights the system's functions and its rich environment. The boxes were meant to zoom into the model by clicking on them. Then a more detailed piece of the model would appear. Zooming would lead in the end to related information, not only the chapters of handbooks, but also related messages, i.e. questions posted by users problems stated by network managers and advice given by system developers.

It was an early attempt to share information before help desks became fashionable. It was one of many attempts to come to grips with the countless aspects the operators and managers of our products were interested in. And of course, we imagined a more appealing user interface, using color, previews and the like.

The method of clicking on a label to zoom-into the labeled content was not new at all, but the conceptual approach was. Here, we considered many of the system-views implied by the system-concept to generate the image.

These views, though explicitly stated in the underlying SGML notation, had to remain implicit in the image. It seemed too complex anyway.

Figure 59: Interactive model of a network subsystem

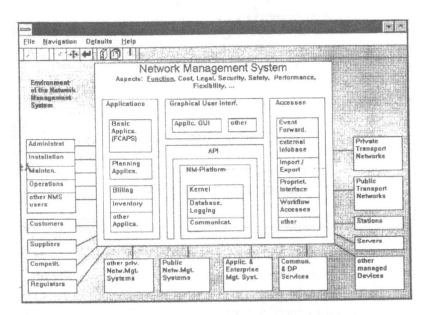

A conceptual model not only provides immediate information by clicking a box, it can also serve as a storage scheme. The label of every clickable box or link in Figures 59 can lead to a collection of documents, images, patents, proposals, data files, messages and other related content. Such documents, thus, have found their proper location in a model which structures a topic's conceptual scope. The model can provide more places to store information than a file cabinet ever could. And we believed a well-designed model could be navigated more quickly and precisely than, say, a collection of handbooks and their tables of content.

This perspective inspired us. We chose the term *macromodel*, because we wanted to break away from the microscopic ways of viewing a system which we have been trained to do as engineers and software developers. We felt a precise but macroscopic view was missing – a kind of holistic perspective which held much detail but did not emphasize it.

We were criticized on two grounds. Macromodels were too coarse, given the endless complexity of communication networks. Second, the models looked good and appealing, but who should build them? Building them seemed to be an art of insiders, not common practice. More than one manager said: "Give me a tool to build macromodels and I'll go along."

Probably they had once been overwhelmed by complexity during their careers. A network not only consisted of thousands of parts, but every part seemed to exist in a dozen versions created over the years and deployed in a network running in some corner of the world.

Even worse: dozens of network variants had been developed for specific countries and even for certain customers to continue operating legacy systems. The number of possible network configurations was, thus, beyond count. Worse still, configurations seemed to multiply since software varied faster than hardware ever could.

Managers knew that certain configuration constraints were not documented. Only some old wizards knew what would happen if an odd constraint was violated and how it could be repaired. What if these wizards retired and their expertise vanished? Was there a way out via macromodels? They seemed promising, but it was too early to tell.

Trying to come to grips with complexity, we tinkered with the matrioshka-principle, which fascinated us. A matrioshka is a hollow wooden puppet with puppets inside – up to seven puppets within puppets.

Our idea was that any system was made up in turn from systems, their components. If we could find an appropriate presentation of a system, it could be used over and over again – for every component, no matter on which level of decomposition and no matter whether hardware or software or else. Such uniformity would make complexity easy to grasp and handle, we guessed.

And any system component would show how it related to many other components – the options of configuration. The relations, thus, had to explain the constraints on versions and variants and we designed them to do just that. It became the first step towards Basic Concepts.

Exotic questions intrigued us on the side: What would it mean to search and browse the Internet via models? What would a conceptual model of Munich, our home town, look like? Would it make sense to conceive Munich as a system?

Macromodels should handle complexity, but they should not be complex themselves. Thus, we determined early on that our models should not be geared to the traditional disciplines of systems research: cybernetics, dynamical systems theory, simulation. Biological and societal systems, too, lay beyond our interest, which included business organizations. And we did not care whether a macromodel would eventually help to compute, simulate or prove anything. If it ever would, then at the end of a long road. The road, however, seemed to start with descriptions in SGML, a precursor of XML.

Testing challenging ideas

We planned to begin with the development of tools. Ideas stretched far. We assessed new ways of representing macromodels and would probably have considered an XML-schema if it had been a viable option at that time. We even considered a knowledge based system, thus reviving the idea of an expert system. In the end we opted to build a new kind of DTD, geared to describe products as systems. We deemed this approach to be viable since Basic Concepts could be expressed in it and editors could handle any DTD. We considered a DTD-driven editor as a sophisticated and practical tool and a first step to more powerful solutions.

Before we started we wanted to test our approach once more. Would it add value to what we got already? Would its users like it and which hidden flaws would emerge?

We decided not to let service personnel test our approach, but engineers responsible for feature development, a most demanding job. Though the term *Feature* remained undefined, it could be anything. Often it turned out to be quite complex like the feature *Call Data Recording*. Feature developers usually had to satisfy customer requirements. One customer required new features of network management for his worldwide corporate network which filled a voluminous document.

We chose feature developers because they had to take many aspects of the entire product into perspective: hardware, software, constraints, versions and the opinions of the sales staff. We guessed they would benefit most from our approach.

Feature developers were the elite – they would not be easy to satisfy. If we wanted to reach them we had to enter their complex world and we tried.

We already mentioned that – before the advent of the Internet – communication systems dealt with calls. Thus we modeled *Call* to show what our approach could accomplish. Figure 60 depicts a few slides we used to explain our call-model to engineers. Though we will not explain the model, it conveys an impression of the modelling issues at stake.

Figure 60: Parts of the Call-model

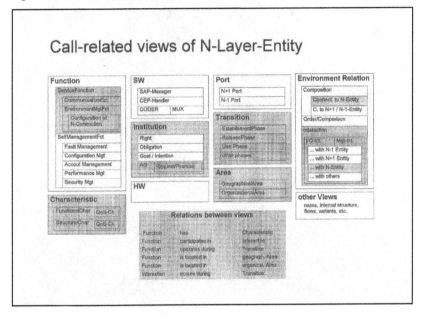

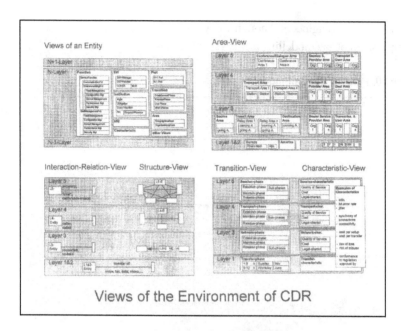

Views of the Environment of CDR

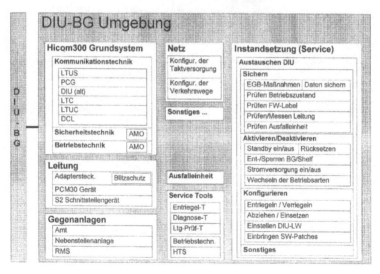

Engineers were interested in views, notably in the views they gained beyond the views available via SDL. For instance, they valued the environment-view (German: Umgebung). One slide shows that even the environment of electronic board DIU-BG was a rich one.

The slides of Figure 60 indicate that – at this stage of modeling – we cared little for formal rigor, but a lot for ontological precision and breadth: We treated all views which mattered – technical and non-technical views alike. And we had fun – we felt we were coming to grips with complexity.

Content in vogue

The Call model was done at a time when attention on content seemed to be in the air. Content management systems had become popular. Repositories were being filled with pieces of information – now called content – and the many opportunities to re-use stored content were touted. In our case, the repository contained the chapters in XML notation of some 200 handbooks. The repository did manage content effectively: it knew the most recent version of any chapter in any language and whether its correctness had been approved. And it was able to aggregate chapters correctly to yield any handbook.

The question, however, how to best capture a large collection of contents never came into focus. Even the once vibrant discipline of knowledge acquisition – a discipline of Artificial Intelligence – had lost its vigor. It had focused on content.

Now, one sales manager told us his problem:

I have a candidate customer who is greatly interested in the network feature Least Cost Routing (LCR). I must provide him with in-depth information before I can make him an offer. LCR, however, is not a cursory feature, it is deeply ingrained in the system and affects and relies on many other features. I assume that LCR has been addressed in many places of our handbooks and, of course, in feature specifications. How can I make sure to find all relevant information and extract it in a coherent manner? I would like to reuse proven information and pass on information which treats all relevant aspects correctly. Can you help me?

We heard about a similar issue from the manager of the training center, who wanted to develop a course on a new and sophisticated feature similar to LCR. He, too, preferred to re-use existing information. Our possibility to help was, however, limited. Of course one could search the handbooks for strings like LCR and extract the chapters where it appeared. But we could not search for content directly since it had not been made explicit. There was no model of the network which contained a model of LCR.

Though we could not help much, these challenges confirmed the idea to concentrate on content, somehow.

The question was: "What if we fill the content management tool with modules of models rather than chapters of handbooks?" Somehow we should be able to aggregate model-modules into a comprehensive model, a macro-model for instance. And we should be able to transform the model into a sequence of chapters and print it as a book. Then we could help the manager of sales to produce information on LCR. We would publish in a content-driven manner.

We would have to enter new terrain and knew about the challenge. Today we would tackle this challenge boldly, having witnessed the great strides made in the BIM domain which we will sketch in Part 3 of the book.

But then we experimented with schemas for modules of content. We built schemas for Basic Concepts and adapted them to our domain. For instance we simplified institutional aspects while elaborating logical ones. And often we sacrificed modularity for practical reasons.

And we provided much leeway when describing systems – the flexibility a DTD naturally provides.

A DTD for systems

The Call-model served its purpose: the engineers understood what we were aiming at, cooperated and agreed on an acid test: to document features in a new way according to our modeling approach.

We had created a SGML DTD (Figure 61) by mapping parts of the tree-type structures of Basic Concepts on the tree-type structures of the DTD. Then we trained authors, offering guidelines and assistance to handle the novel documentation tool.

But our story ends there. It does not end because we had taken the wrong approach and finally had to give up. It ends, because the world changed. Internet technology was about to replace the technology which handles calls. The communications industry, thus, changed fundamentally and the modelling team dispersed.

Figure 61: Model-based Feature Documentation

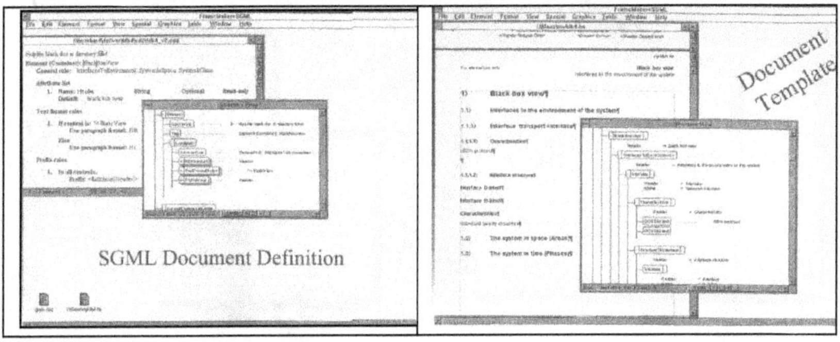

SGML Document Definition

Recent approaches to model building

A few years later, new approaches to modeling were underway. The MatML Working Group (1999-2001) began to work on material systems, and in the early years of the new millennium work on the Systems Modeling Language (SysML) commenced. It is a general-purpose graphical modeling language for specifying, analyzing, designing, and verifying complex systems that may include hardware, software, information, personnel, procedures, and facilities [sysML (2017)]. Being similar in style to UML, sysML models, for instance, use cases, requirements, activities, state machines and blocks.

A Block is a modular unit that describes the structure of a system or element. It may represent structural and behavioral features, properties, ports, flows (of data, material, or energy), operations and system states. The parts of a system can be described by blocks, used to describe anything.

Industry specific approaches

While sysML does not cater to a certain industry or application, other approaches do – also beginning in the new millennium. Examples in case are modeling languages for the production industry (PLM) and the construction industry (BIM). They do not specialize the sysML approach: they take original approaches.

In Part 3 of the book we highlight the BIM approach and sketch the PLM, approach, both of which we deem novel and powerful. And we marvel at the tools they made possible.

Part 3: Modern Models

Part 3

Modern Models

Part 3: Modern Models

9

Concepts of a Vast Domain

After we had quit the work on modeling in the network-domain, exciting news about the domain of Building Information Management (BIM) reached us: an audacious modeling effort was underway, orders of magnitude bigger than what we had envisioned. Models should cater to the worldwide construction industry, to all sorts of building, all phases of a building's lifecycle and to the many sorts of actor involved.

We have already mentioned BIM on and off. Now we will look closer to its conceptual core of openBIM since concept design will affect all who build and use tools for design (CAD), engineering (CAE), manufacturing (CAM) and lifecycle management (PLM).

The number and scope of concepts for the entire industry had to be enormous. Precision is required as well: models must allow to evaluate a building's cost, feasibility, safety, usability, energy efficiency, conformity etc. Many specialists share their knowledge of a building – designs and evaluations – thus contributing to a pool of models of a building.

Naturally, we will concentrate on the domain's core of concepts. Their name *Industry Foundation Classes* has been well chosen. They convey the conceptual variety the domain demands, and they demonstrate the kind of task which had awaited us, had we developed tools for communication networks.

Industry Foundation Classes (IFC)

The standard ISO 16739:2013 defines Industry Foundation Classes (IFC4) for sharing data and models in the construction and facility management industries. The organization BuildingSMART International Ltd. (bSI) promotes these efforts and has posted results in the public domain [bSI (2017)].

Note that we will use the term *IFC* also to refer to the organization bSI. We will not distinguish between bSI, IFC, IFC4, OpenBIM and BIM since we are interested mainly in BIM as a domain and in IFC as the source of concepts to capture BIM. In this sense we will use *IFC* and *BIM*.

IFC's large XML-schema of some 14,000 lines of code captures our interest because it standardizes some 800 key domain concepts. Models and tools – much of the BIM endeavor – build on them. We will try to convey an impression of these concepts and thus of the IFC approach which, of course, contrasts with our approach.

Figure 62 lists several layers of concepts, the idea being that the concepts of a lower layer help define the concepts or descriptions of a higher layer. IFC puts the layering idea like this:

Resource layer — the lowest layer includes all individual schemas containing resource definitions. Those definitions do not include a globally unique identifier and shall not be used independently of a definition declared at a higher layer;

Core layer — this layer includes the kernel schema and the core extension schemas, containing the most general entity definitions, all entities defined at the core layer, or above carry a globally unique ID and optionally owner and history information (*IfcOwnerHistory*);

Interoperability layer — this layer includes schemas containing entity definitions that are specific to a general product, process or resource specialization used across several disciplines, those definitions are typically utilized for inter-domain exchange and sharing of construction information;

Domain layer — the highest layer includes schemas containing entity definitions that are specializations of products, processes or resources specific to a certain discipline, those definitions are typically utilized for intra-domain exchange and sharing of information.

Figure 62: Excerpt of IFC's layers of concepts

Layer	Example Content
Domain Layer	• Building Controls Domain • Plumbing FireProtection Domain • Structural Elements Domain • Structural Analysis Domain • Heating, Ventilation and Air Conditioning (HVAC) Domain • Electrical Domain • Architecture Domain • Construction Management Domain, etc.
Interoperability Layer	• Services Elements • Component Elements • Building Elements • Management Elements • Facilities Elements
Core Layer	• Kernel • Control Extensions • Product Extensions • Process Extensions
Resource Layer	• DateTime Resource • Material Resource • Geometry Resource • Profile Resource • Property Resource • Quantity Resource • Appearance Resource • Representation Resource • Constraint Resource • Structural Load Resource • Cost Resource, etc.

It is impossible for us to trace out the conceptual scope of BIM. We are not familiar with buildings, construction and the technologies and vocabularies involved. Most readers will be BIM-unaware as well.

And we cannot do justice to all the challenges inherent in the BIM domain – the language problem for instance. While we dealt with technical documentation in six natural languages, the BIM industry should be open to most any language. Also we never had to pay attention to national standards. Building designs, however, should conform to local standards which, by the way, often define terminology.

IFC, fortunately, is meticulously documented on IFC's website, using various notations and compilations – even an ontology.

We will focus on IFC's approach to conceptual modeling which starts with concept design, covers schema design and leads to model design.

Generic concepts

The Layers mentioned in Figure 62 are not layers of abstraction. Nevertheless, the IFC-schema makes ample use of abstraction and inheritance. We will, therefore, consider some highly abstract concepts first. *IfcObject* resides close to the top of the hierarchy of domain concepts. It inherits from the concept *Root* which carries information used for housekeeping.

What is an object? IFC says: An *IfcObject* is the generalization of any semantically treated thing or process. This comes close to our notion of a system.

The following figures show that little can be said about the concept *IfcObject* except that it may inherit a definition. The relation *IfcRelDefinesByType* relates an object-occurrence with its defining type *IfcTypeObject*.

Figure 63: IfcObject

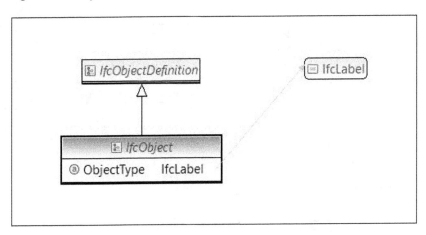

An IfcTypeObject (Figure 66) serves to inherit properties, respectively ordered sets of properties. We will not touch on the finesses of the logic of inheritance. Suffice it to say that, eventually, objects carry domain-specific information in form of inherited or individually specified properties which are similar to system-characteristics.

Figure 64: IfcRoot

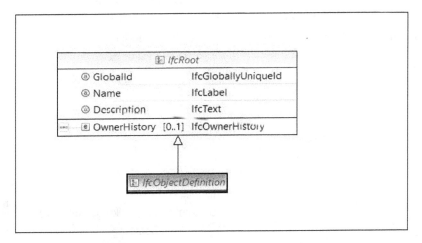

Figure 65: IfcRelDefinesByType

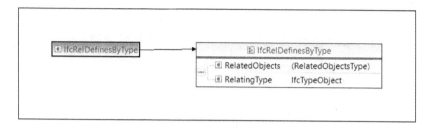

Figure 66: IfcTypeObject

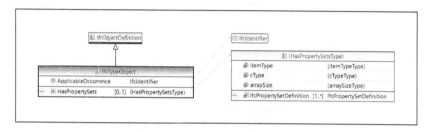

Abstraction and refinement, generalization and specialization, typing and instantiation have been key means of description in any domain.

Figure 67 sketches a sample hierarchy of concepts leading to the specific concept Door-17. It is constructed from concepts defined by the IFC-schema and may have been individually refined by a model builder.

Figure 67: Example of a class hierarchy

```
Root
     ObjectDefinition
             Object, TypeObject
                   Product, TypeProduct
                         Element, ElementType
                               BuildingElement, BuildingElementType
                               Door, DoorType
                               [instance Door-17]
```

There are seven fundamental entity types in the IFC model, which are derived from *IfcObject*. They form the 2nd level of specialization within the IFC class hierarchy under the object branch.

Figure 68: Kinds of objects

- **products** – are physical objects (manufactured, supplied or created) for incorporation into a project. They may be physically existing or tangible. Products may be defined by shape representations and have a location in the coordinate space.
- **processes** – are actions taking place in a project with the intent of, e.g., acquiring, constructing, or maintaining objects. Processes are placed in sequence in time.
- **controls** – are concepts that control or constrain other objects. Controls can be seen as guide, specification, regulation, constraint or other requirement applied to an object that has to be fulfilled.
- **resources** – are concepts that describe the use of an object mainly within a process.
- **actors** – are human agents that are involved in a project during its full life cycle.
- **project** – Is the undertaking of some engineering activities leading towards a product. (derived from *IfcObjectDefinition*)
- **group** – Is an arbitrary collection of objects.

A few generic examples will introduce to the world of IFC's concepts:

Figure 69: IfcProduct

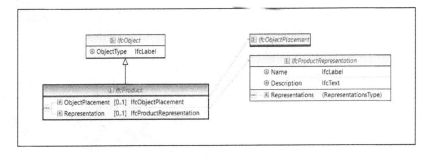

Figure 70: IfcElement

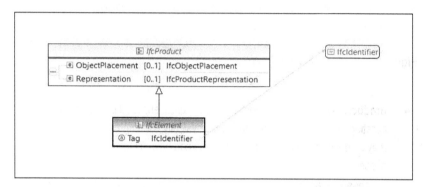

Figure 71: IfcDoor

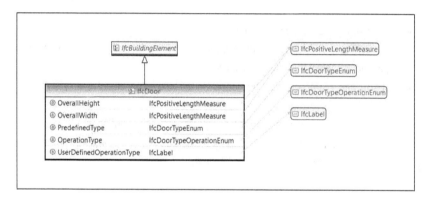

Figure 71 shows a few of the properties applying to doors. They substantiate the fact that in practice one must deal with numerous kinds of door, each implementing a special combination of properties.

What is a property? Similar to what we said about system-characteristics, a property is everything but an object and a relation. Also, properties should describe something. Names and IDs, by the way, do not describe.

Figure 72: IfcDoorLiningProperties

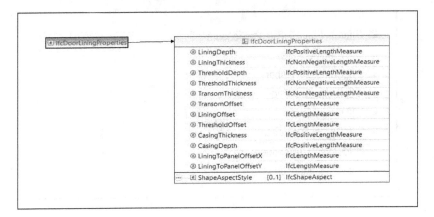

Figure 73 lists a number of properties which do not describe domain-properties but formal properties used to represent domain-properties, e.g. in form of an enumeration, list or table of values. We are well advised to distinguish domain-properties such as DoorLinigProperties from the properties of representation.

Figure 73: Formal properties (Examples)

- IfcComplexProperty
- IfcSimpleProperty
  - o   IfcPropertyBoundedValue
  - o   IfcPropertyEnumeratedValue
  - o   IfcPropertyListValue
  - ○   IfoPropertyReferenceValue
  - o   IfcPropertySingleValue
  - o   IfcPropertyTableValue

The XML-schema *Property Set Definition* (PSD) defines such properties. Other specifications, like Data Types (Figure 74), we can only touch on. They are well documented by IFC.

121

Figure 74: Data types (Examples)

- IfcAmountOfSubstanceMeasure
- IfcAreaMeasure
- IfcComplexNumber
- IfcContextDependentMeasure
- IfcCountMeasure
- IfcDescriptiveMeasure
- IfcElectricCurrentMeasure
- IfcLengthMeasure

Relations

Mainly two means of description carry domain-related information: the properties of objects and the relations between objects. There is no additional information hidden in hierarchies of concepts since classification algorithms can generate taxonomies, at least in principle.

Our approach does not differ in that matter: The characteristics and re-lations of systems carry the information. Only our named views add infor-mation not present in the IFC scheme. Algorithms cannot generate this kind of information unless they understand the domain.

The IFC-schema defines approximately 50 different types of relation-ships, grouped into six fundamental types of relationships listed in Figure 76.

Note that only three types express genuine domain-information: Assign-ment, Decomposition and Connectivity. The others deal with issues of repre-sentation such as *IfcRelDefinition*, which we discussed. One may say, three types of relations – namely RelAssigns, RelConnects and RelDecomposes – are of an ontological nature, the rest is of a representational nature. Relations – like RelAssociatesDocument – serve information management. All relations inherit from the concept *IfcRelationship*.

IFC characterizes its main types of relations like this:

Figure 75: Types of relationship

- **Assignment** – Is a generalization of "link" relationships among instances of objects and its various subtypes. A link denotes the specific association through which one object (the client) applies the services of other objects (the suppliers), or through which one object may navigate to other objects.

- **Connectivity** – handles the connectivity of objects.

- **Decomposition** – defines the general concept of elements being composed or decomposed. The decomposition relationship denotes a whole/part hierarchy with the ability to navigate from the whole (the composition) to the parts and vice versa.

- **Association** – refers to external sources of information (most notably a classification, library or document) and associates it to objects or property definitions.

- **Definition** – uses a type definition or property set definition (seen as partial type information) to define the properties of the object instance. It is a specific - occurrence relationship

- **Declaration** – handles the link between object definitions and property definitions and the declaring context

Figure 76 lists the relations defined by the IFC-schema.

Figure 76: Relations defined by the Ifc-Schema

IfcRelAssigns
IfcRelAssignsToActor
IfcRelAssignsToControl
IfcRelAssignsToGroup
IfcRelAssignsToGroupByFactor
IfcRelAssignsToProcess
IfcRelAssignsToProduct
IfcRelAssignsToResource

IfcRelAssociates
IfcRelAssociatesApproval
IfcRelAssociatesClassification
IfcRelAssociatesConstraint
IfcRelAssociatesDocument
IfcRelAssociatesLibrary
IfcRelAssociatesMaterial

IfcRelConnects
IfcRelSpaceBoundary
IfcRelServicesBuildings
IfcRelSequence
IfcRelReferencedInSpatialStructure
IfcRelInterferesElements
IfcRelFlowControlElements
IfcRelFillsElement
IfcRelConnectsElements
IfcRelConnectsPathElements
IfcRelConnectsPortToElement
IfcRelConnectsPorts
IfcRelConnectsStructuralActivity
IfcRelConnectsStructuralMember
IfcRelConnectsWithEccentricity
IfcRelConnectsWithRealizingElements
IfcRelContainedInSpatialStructure
IfcRelCoversBldgElements
IfcRelCoversSpaces

IfcRelDecomposes
IfcRelAggregates
IfcRelVoidsElement
IfcRelProjectsElement
IfcRelNests

IfcRelDeclares

IfcRelDefines
IfcRelDefinesByObject
IfcRelDefinesByProperties
IfcRelDefinesByTemplate
IfcRelDefinesByType

124

A Glimpse of the low down

So far we have sketched generic concepts only. Now we will get into some detail via examples – an eclectic and non-representative choice of examples. Their notations remain un-explained, but they still convey a flavour of what is involved. Finally, the example models of a clinic and a heating device will show the use of concepts in practice.

RelAssignsToActor – an Example

Figure 77 sketches the relation of type *IfcRelAssigns* and shows that assignment can be constrained: an object of a certain kind can only be related to object types which are enumerated. The relation *RelAssignsToActor* is an instance in case. Figure 78 says that an actor is an organization, a person or both. Actors have roles and Figure 81 enumerates them.

Figure 77: Definition of RelAssigns

```
<xs:complexType name="IfcRelAssigns" abstract="true">
<xs:complexContent>
<xs:extension base="ifc:IfcRelationship">
<xs:sequence>
<xs:element name="RelatedObjects">
<xs:complexType>
<xs:sequence>
<xs:element ref="ifc:IfcObjectDefinition" maxOccurs="unbounded"/>
</xs:sequence>
<xs:attribute ref="ifc:itemType" fixed="ifc:IfcObjectDefinition"/>
<xs:attribute ref="ifc:cType" fixed="set"/>
<xs:attribute ref="ifc:arraySize" use="optional"/>
</xs:complexType>
</xs:element>
</xs:sequence>
<xs:attribute    name="RelatedObjectsType"    type="ifc:IfcObjectTypeEnum"
use="optional"/>
</xs:extension> </xs:complexContent> </xs:complexType> ...
```

Figure 78: Definition of RelAssignsToActor (Excerpt)

```
<xs:element name="IfcRelAssignsToActor"/> ....
   <xs:sequence>
    <xs:element name=  "RelatingActor"  type="ifc:IfcActor"/>
    <xs:element name=   "ActingRole"    type="ifc:IfcActorRole"/>
   </xs:sequence>
```

Figure 79: Definition of Actor (Excerpt)

```
<xs:element name="IfcActor"/>
    <xs:element name="TheActor">
    <xs:complexType>
     <xs:group ref="ifc:IfcActorSelect"/>
<xs:group name="IfcActorSelect">
  <xs:choice>
   <xs:element ref="ifc:IfcOrganization"/>
   <xs:element ref="ifc:IfcPerson"/>
   <xs:element ref="ifc:IfcPersonAndOrganization"/>
   </xs:choice>
```

Figure 80: Definition of ActorRole (Excerpt)

```
<xs:element name="IfcActorRole"/>
 <xs:complexType name="IfcActorRole">
  <xs:complexContent>
   <xs:extension base="ifc:Entity">
    <xs:attribute name="Role" type="ifc:IfcRoleEnum" use="optional"/>
```

Figure 81: Enumeration of Actor-roles

```
<xs:simpleType name="IfcRoleEnum">
  <xs:restriction base="xs:string">
  <xs:enumeration value="supplier"/>
  <xs:enumeration value="manufacturer"/>
  <xs:enumeration value="contractor"/>
   [list of values]...
  </xs:restriction>
 </xs:simpleType>
```

ValveType – an Example

After looking at a specific relation we consider a specific object *Valve*. Figure 82 positions the concept in a simplified taxonomy.

Figure 82: Conceptual embedding of *Valve*

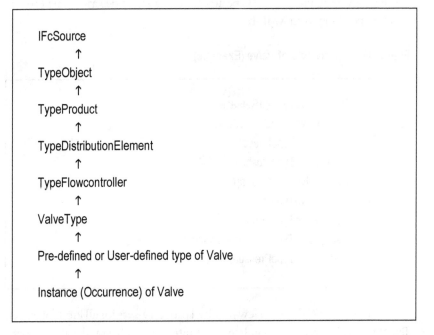

IFcSource
↑
TypeObject
↑
TypeProduct
↑
TypeDistributionElement
↑
TypeFlowcontroller
↑
ValveType
↑
Pre-defined or User-defined type of Valve
↑
Instance (Occurrence) of Valve

IfcValveType defines information commonly shared by occurrences of valves, i.e. instances of *IfcValve*. Several types of information (see Figure 83) can be shared and we will look at some of them.

Figure 83: Types of information about valves

- Properties
- Representations of shape
- Materials
- Composition of elements
- Ports
- Assigned process types

Properties

The property set definitions (Pset) according to Figure 84 are applicable to this entity via the Pre-definedType attribute: Figure 85 describes one PropertySet by pointing to an XML-file

Figure 84:Property sets of *Valve* (Example)

- Pset_ValveTypeAirRelease
- Pset_ValveTypeDrawOffCock
- Pset_ValveTypeFaucet
- Pset_ValveTypeFlushing
- Pset_ValveTypeGasTap
- Pset_ValveTypeIsolating
- Pset_ValveTypeMixing
- Pset_ValveTypePressureReducing
- Pset_ValveTypePressureRelief

Note that IFC defines a few hundred property-sets for all kinds of object. But there will never be a complete set of internationally standardized attributes. IFC defined property sets with the intent to standardize a basic set of properties, whereas other property sets can be regionally defined, or agreed upon in projects.

Figure 85: Pset_ValveTypeAirRelease

Applicable Entity	IfcValve/AIRRELEASE
Definition	Valve used to release air from a pipe or fitting. Note that an air release valve is constrained to have a single port pattern.
XML Specification	Pset_ValveTypeAirRelease.xml

Material

The material of the IfcValveType is defined by the RelatingMaterial attribute on the IfcRelAssociatesMaterial relationship. The following keywords should be used:

- 'Body'. The primary material from which the object is constructed.
- 'Operation'. Material from which the operating mechanism (gate, globe, plug, needle, clack etc.) of the valve is constructed.

Ports

The distribution ports relating to the IfcValveType type are defined by IfcDistributionPort and attached by the relationship IfcRelConnectsPortToElement

Relations

ValveType – like any type of object or product – can relate in the many ways. In this example relations tell the valve is made of a certain material, shared the properties of a certain type and has a port to release air:

- IfcRelAssociatesMaterial
- IfcRelDefinesByType
- IfcRelConnectsPortToElement

On spatial structure

Figure 86 indicates how varied spatial modelling techniques are for the BIM-domain. [Borrmann (2015)] describes the details.

Figure 86: Techniques of Geometrical Description

Object	Means of spatial description
IfcElement	Product Placement, Box Geometry, FootPrint Geometry, Body SurfaceOrSolidModel Geometry, Body SurfaceModel Geometry, Body Tessellation Geometry, Body Brep Geometry, Body AdvancedBrep Geometry, Body CSG Geometry, Mapped Geometry
IfcDistributionFlowElement	Axis Geometry, Clearance Geometry, Lighting Geometry

We have not emphasized the significance of connectivity in our scheme, although one of the purposes of a communication network is to achieve connectivity. The reason is that interaction usually implies some form of connection and composition as well. Physical connectors were not an issue.

The BIM-domain differs with respect to the connectivity of objects in 3D space. Walls and rooms must connect seamlessly, pipes and cables connect as well, doors must fill spaces, etc. Figure 87 contains some ways to express connections.

The need for sets of relations as a means of structuring seems to be a minor one in the BIM domain. Here, a powerful structuring principle prevails: the geometrical and topological structure of a building in 2D or 3D space. The layout in space often implies order, composition and interaction. Floors are ordered from ground floor to top floor. Rooms are components of a floor. And adjacent rooms naturally interact, exchanging heat and sound.

Figure 87: Relations of an ElectricMotor (Examples)

Relation	Example
RelFillsElement	The element *Motor* fills the void element *PowerCabin*
RelConnectsElements	Motor connects to the Element *PowerLine*
RelInterferesElements	The element *Motor* puts a load on element *FloorSlab*
RelProjectsElement	The element *Motor* has the feature *Not-removable.*
RelVoidsElement	The element *Motor* requires the Void *Door-opening*
RelConnectsWithRealizingElements	The element *Motor* generates the FlowElement *Electric- current*
RelConnectsElements	The element *Motor* connects to the element *StandbyPowerSupply*
RelContainedInSpatialStructure	The element *Motor is contained* in the spatial structure element *MachineRoom.*
RelCoversBldgElements	The BuildingElement *MachineRoom* covers the Element *Motor.*

These examples of relations and static products like valve or motor neglect dynamic aspects which in turn are treated by the generic concept *Process* and its subtypes like *Event, Procedure* and *Task.*

Many other topics of interest will not be treated adequately either, Model Views for instance. A model view defines the selection of information about a building which is needed by a given expert at a given phase of a building's lifecycle, e.g. by an engineer concerned with structural analysis. A Model View Definition (MVD) filters the entire model as to objects, relations and properties.

Our approach did not address the lifecycle of a network nor did it cater to many different specialists. We fed information to only one sink: the service personnel and we gathered information from one source: the team of network developers.

Architects, engineers, builders and facility managers crucially depend on spatial structure. This peculiarity is not the case in the domains of networks and organizations. Otherwise our concept of structure would have been a different one.

Many relations of type IfcRelConnects can specify how elements relate in space, e.g. whether boundaries or ports connect.

Concepts about Space

Spatial representation tends to dominate BIM-models. For a detailed description see [Borrmann (2015)]. Numerous concepts deal with space, structure and form. Figures 88 to 90 show a selection of them. They indicate the descriptive refinement required by BIM and achieved by IFC.

Figure 88: Concepts describing space (Selection)

- IfcSpatialElement
- IfcSpatialStructureElement
- IfcExternalSpatialElement
- IfcSpatialZone
- IfcSpace
- IfcRelatingSpace
- StructuralSurfaceMember
- IfcStructuralConnection
- IfcStructuralConnectionCondition
- IfcRelConnectsStructuralActivity
- IfcRelSpaceBoundary
- IfcRelCoversSpaces
- IfcRelConnectsStructuralMember
- IfcRelContainedInSpatialStructure

Part 3: Modern Models

Figure 89: Characteristics of Spatial Structure (Example)

```
<xs:simpleType name="IfcElementCompositionEnum">
  <xs:restriction base="xs:string">
  <xs:enumeration value="complex"/>
  <xs:enumeration value="element"/>
  <xs:enumeration value="partial"/>
  <xs:enumeration value="junction"/>
  <xs:enumeration value="obstruction"/>
```

Figure 90: Descriptive detail of a boundary (Excerpt)

```
<xs:element name="IfcBoundaryEdgeCondition"/>
<xs:sequence>
    <xs:element name="TranslationalStiffnessByLengthX">
        <xs:group     ref="ifc:IfcModulusOfTranslationalSubgradeReactionSe-
lect"/>
    <xs:element name="TranslationalStiffnessByLengthY">
        <xs:group     ref="ifc:IfcModulusOfTranslationalSubgradeReactionSe-
lect"/>
    <xs:element name="TranslationalStiffnessByLengthZ">
        <xs:group     ref="ifc:IfcModulusOfTranslationalSubgradeReactionSe-
lect"/>
    <xs:element name="RotationalStiffnessByLengthX">
        <xs:group ref="ifc:IfcModulusOfRotationalSubgradeReactionSelect"/>
    <xs:element name="RotationalStiffnessByLengthY">
        <xs:group ref="ifc:IfcModulusOfRotationalSubgradeReactionSelect"/>
    <xs:element name="RotationalStiffnessByLengthZ">
        <xs:group ref="ifc:IfcModulusOfRotationalSubgradeReactionSelect"/>
</xs:sequence>
```

Liebich [Liebich (2009)] provides a more complete rendition of IFC-means to model structure, spatial structure and connectivity in particular.

133

The IFC-notion of system

At last, we will have a look at the IFC concept *System* and its subtype *Zone* (Figure 91). Both are significant means to model structure and function, extending the means provided by relations between objects. IFC conceives a system differently from the way we have done. It will pay off to study the concept, because handling structure and function is an important and challenging issue. IFC defines a system (IfcSystem) as follows:

- A system is an organized combination of related parts within an AEC product, composed for a common purpose or function or to provide a service. A system is essentially a functionally related aggregation of products. The grouping relationship to one or several instances of IfcProduct (the system members) is handled by IfcRelAssignsToGroup.

- The use of *IfcSystem* often applies to the representation of building services related systems, such as the piping system, cold water system, etc. Members within such a system may or may not be connected using the connectivity related entities (through IfcDistributionPort).

- Reference to the spatial structure via the objectified relationship IfcRelServicesBuildings, which is serviced by the system.

- The propertySet *Service Life Factors* captures various factors that impact the expected service life of elements within the system or zone, e.g. Quality of Components, Design Level, Work Execution Level, Indoor Environment, etc.

Figure 91: Supertypes and subtypes of IfcSystem

```
Root
      ObjectDefinition
          Object
          Group
              System
                  BuildingSystem
                  DistributionSystem
                  StructureAnalysisModel
                  Zone
```

A concept designer wrote about systems [Liebich (2009)]:

Within the IFC Model, a system is defined as a subtype of IfcGroup. That is, it acts as a functional related aggregation of objects. However, whilst the IfcGroup can aggregate any set of instances that are subtypes of IfcObject, the IfcSystem can be restricted by a WHERE rule (see Figure 92) so that it can only aggregate subtypes of IfcElement or other (sub-) systems.

Whilst this allows for any subtype of element to participate in an IfcSystem, the definition that they should be related is significant. Typically, an IfcSystem will act for a particular purpose and the elements that are aggregated into the system should be consistent with that purpose. For instance, in an architectural context, a system might be used to define a functionally related set of walls. In structural engineering, this might be beams and columns whilst in a building services context, a IFC system will comprise distribution elements (pipes or ducts or cables and related items). Objects that are clearly intended for use within one purpose should not be mixed in a system with objects that are clearly intended for a different purpose.

In general, it is expected that the elements that comprise a system will be connected together in a 'systematic' way. However, there is no enforcement of a connectivity requirement within IfcSystem. Therefore, if there is a need for elements to be connected (e.g. to establish a flow path), this has to be defined prior ... or be determined by applying external rules or procedures ...

Figure 92: Example Rule

```
ENTITY IfcSystem

SUBTYPE OF (IfcGroup);
INVERSE
ServicesBuildings : SET [0:1] OF IfcRelServicesBuildings FOR RelatingSystem;
WHERE
WR1 : SIZEOF (QUERY (temp <* SELF\IfcGroup.IsGroupedBy.RelatedObjects |
NOT (('IFCPRODUCTEXTENSION.IFCELEMENT' IN TYPEOF(temp)) OR
('IFCPRODUCTEXTENSION.IFCSYSTEM' IN TYPEOF(temp)))
)) = 0; END_ENTITY;
```

Liebich uses the terms *purpose* and *function* to explain the meaning of *IfcSystem*. Though the view *function* is highly significant for all technical artifacts, it remains implicit, expressed in prose. In this context, IFC also defines *IfcZone*, a kind of *IfcSystem*, dedicated to space and function.

A zone is a group of spaces, partial spaces or other zones. Zone structures may not be hierarchical (contrary to the spatial structure of a project – see *IfcSpatialStructureElement*), i.e. one individual IfcSpace may be associated with zero, one, or several IfcZone's. IfcSpaces are grouped into an IfcZone by using the objectified relationship IfcRelAssignsToGroup as specified at the supertype *IfcGroup*.

These and the following statements reveal considerations concept designers deal with. They also seem to convey the need to refine the concept *system*, e.g. by introducing the concept *spatial system*, in order to extend the means to describe function:

- In some building service use cases the zone denotes a view-based delimited volume for the purpose of analysis and calculation.
- An IfcZone is a spatial system under which individual IfcSpace's (and other IfcZone's) are grouped. In contrary to the IfcSpatialZone entity, IfcZone is a mere grouping, it cannot define an own geometric representation and placement.
- The IfcZone is regarded as the spatial system (as compared to the building service, electrical, or analytical system).
- One of the purposes of a zone is to define a fire compartment. In this case it defines the geometric information about the fire compartment (through the contained spaces) and information, whether this compartment is ventilated or sprinkler protected. In addition the fire risk code and the hazard type can be added, the coding is normally defined within a national fire regulation.

The next chapter sketches two models. Note that the model of a clinic, though highly structured, does not use the concept IfcSystem. The second model of a device describes a system in detail.

10

Sample Models

IFC-model of a clinic

The following example describes a clinic in a form complying with the IFC standard. We thank the unknown supplier of the model. We have used four files conforming to the schema IFC2x3, precursor of the IFC4 standard. They are between 12 MB and 200 MB in size, containing up to 3,2 million lines of code per file. The model has been created via a commercial CAD system.

This example, as well as the following, should convey prime features of an IFC-model of a technical artifact. We will not discuss any technical aspect, merely the model's characteristics.

Figure 93 presents an outside view of a part of the clinic, Figure 95 a look inside, Figure 97 a comprehensive view.

Figures 94, 96 and 98 present the model's concepts, corresponding to Figures 93, 95 and 97 respectively. According to Figure 94, the model describes 738 beams, 195 columns and diverse entities, and contains 9714 relations, most of them used to ascribe properties to objects. Few relations deal with functional or spatial composition.

Figure 93: Beams, columns and slabs-1

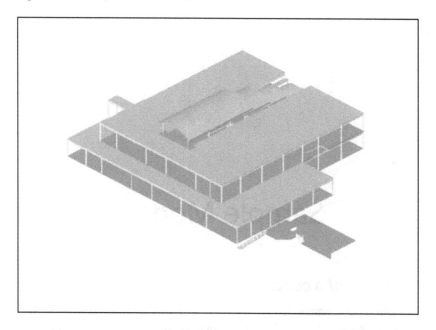

The frequent relations of type RelSpaceBoundary describe which elements, e.g. walls, connect in space and which ConnectionGeometry applies. The also numerous relations of type IfcRelConnectsPathElements serve a similar purpose. IFC states:

> *IfcRelConnectsPathElements provides the connectivity information between two elements, which have path information – the information required to describe the connection between two path based elements that might have single or multiple layers of material. It specifies where at the path based element a connection is given (at the start, in the middle or at the end).*

Figure 94: Beams, columns and slabs-2

Entity	Amount
⊟ **Entities**	**1101**
IfcBeam	738
IfcBuilding	1
IfcBuildingStorey	4
IfcColumn	195
IfcFooting	96
IfcOpeningElement	7
IfcProject	1
IfcRailing	3
IfcRamp	1
IfcRampFlight	1
IfcRoof	12
IfcSite	1
IfcSlab[Floor]	6
IfcSlab[Roof]	7
IfcStair	1
IfcStairFlight	1
IfcWallStandardCase	26
⊟ **Relations**	**9714**
IfcRelAggregates	12
IfcRelAssociatesMaterial	46
IfcRelConnectsPathElements	28
IfcRelContainedInSpatialStructure	4
IfcRelDefinesByProperties	9588
IfcRelDefinesByType	29
IfcRelVoidsElement	7
⊟ **EntityTypes**	**1**
IFCCOLUMNTYPE	29

In Figure 96, the frequent concept *IFCMember* refers to structural elements like posts, purlins, studs, etc. The frequent concept *IfcRelSpaceBoundary* handles the relationship between an element and the space bounding the element. Many such relationships may apply to an element.

139

Figure 95: Walls, spaces and openings-1

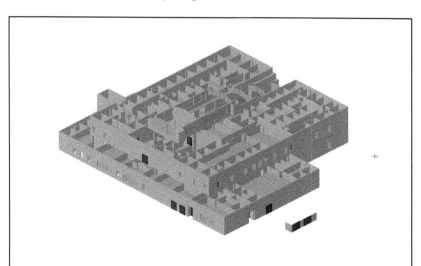

Figure 97 depicts some of the clinic's technical subsystems and Figure 98 lists the concepts used to model them. The listed EntityTypes mention the functions of infrastructure, e.g. sanitation, electricity, cooling, lighting and fire suppression.

One would imagine that the plant depicted in Figures 97 abounds with architectural, functional and technical systems and subsystems. The concept IfcSystem, however, does not appear in Figure 98.

Figures 99 and 100 show part of the pipes, ducts, flow segments, etc. that make up a clinic's infrastructure. Distribution systems, ducts and flows, ports and port-connections play a major role.

Most Figures depict elaborate structures and indicate the importance of means to design, represent and evaluate structure. Here, the figures present structure in space rather than structures of function.

The next model will deal more with the functional side of structure.

Figure 96: Walls, spaces and openings-2

Entity	Amount
⊟ **Entities**	**3299**
IfcBuilding	1
IfcBuildingStorey	4
IfcCovering	250
IfcCurtainWall	31
IfcDoor	254
IfcFlowTerminal	102
IfcFurnishingElement	118
IfcMember	534
IfcOpeningElement	403
IfcPlate	172
IfcProject	1
IfcRailing	9
IfcSite	1
IfcSlab[Landing]	3
IfcSpace	269
IfcStair	3
IfcStairFlight	6
IfcWall	15
IfcWallStandardCase	1065
IfcWindow	58
⊟ **Relations**	**22567**
IfcRelAggregates	40
IfcRelAssociatesMaterial	1333
IfcRelConnectsPathElements	2103
IfcRelContainedInSpatialStructure	80
IfcRelDefinesByProperties	14701
IfcRelDefinesByType	481
IfcRelFillsElement	302
IfcRelSpaceBoundary	3124
IfcRelVoidsElement	403

Figure 97: Comprehensive view 1

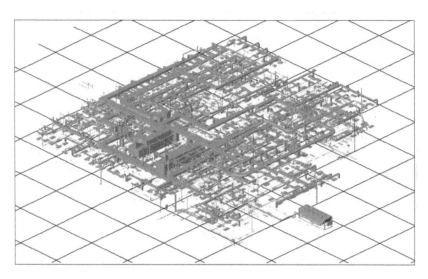

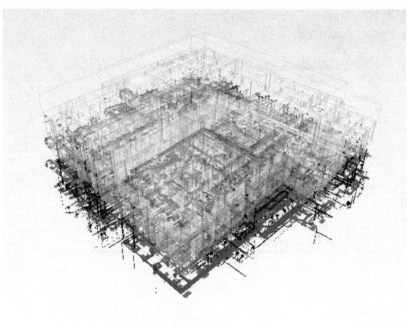

Figure 98: Comprehensive view 2

Entity	Amount
Entities	**16545**
IfcBuilding	1
IfcBuildingStorey	4
IfcEnergyConversionDevice	3
IfcFlowController	173
IfcFlowFitting	6693
IfcFlowMovingDevice	137
IfcFlowSegment	5952
IfcFlowStorageDevice	1
IfcFlowTerminal	3053
IfcProject	1
IfcSite	1
IfcSpace	526
Relations	**118742**
IfcRelAggregates	6
IfcRelContainedInSpatialStructure	265
IfcRelDefinesByProperties	111260
IfcRelDefinesByType	7211
EntityTypes	**16**
IFCAIRTERMINALTYPE	13
IFCCHILLERTYPE	1
IFCDUCTFITTINGTYPE	796
IFCDUCTSEGMENTTYPE	1703
IFCELECTRICAPPLIANCETYPE	3
IFCFANTYPE	8
IFCFIRESUPPRESSIONTERMINALTYPE	1
IFCLIGHTFIXTURETYPE	9
IFCOUTLETTYPE	2
IFCPIPEFITTINGTYPE	408
IFCPIPESEGMENTTYPE	4249
IFCPUMPTYPE	1
IFCSANITARYTERMINALTYPE	9
IFCTANKTYPE	1
IFCTRANSFORMERTYPE	1
IFCVALVETYPE	6

Figure 99: Flow-related elements 1

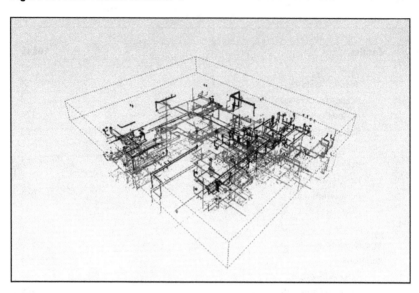

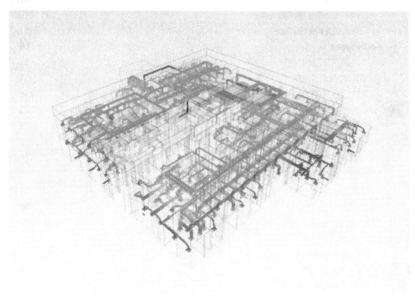

Figure 100: Flow related elements 2

Entity	Amount
⊟ **Entities**	**19651**
IfcBuilding	1
IfcBuildingStorey	3
IfcDistributionPort	13058
IfcFlowController	254
IfcFlowFitting	3318
IfcFlowMovingDevice	2
IfcFlowSegment	2893
IfcFlowStorageDevice	1
IfcFlowTerminal	119
IfcProject	1
IfcSite	1
⊟ **Relations**	**78888**
IfcRelAggregates	3
IfcRelAssociatesClassification	394
IfcRelAssociatesMaterial	1
IfcRelConnectsPorts	6529
IfcRelConnectsPortToElement	13058
IfcRelContainedInSpatialStructure	3
IfcRelDefinesByProperties	58500
IfcRelDefinesByType	400
⊟ **EntityTypes**	**7**
IFCFANTYPE	1
IFCPIPEFITTINGTYPE	372
IFCPIPESEGMENTTYPE	6
IFCPUMPTYPE	1
IFCSANITARYTERMINALTYPE	9
IFCTANKTYPE	1
IFCVALVETYPE	10

IFC-model of a device

This example describes a device in a form complying with the standard IFC4. Figures 101 and 102 sketch a heat pump radiator in terms of its main components and their connections. Arrow heads indicate ports and flows.

Figure 105 lists the concepts used to model the device. There are, for instance, 18 pipe segments of two different kinds, the PipeSegmentTypes, linked via two kinds of fittings, the PipeFittingTypes.

Figure 101: Front view of HeatPumpRadiator

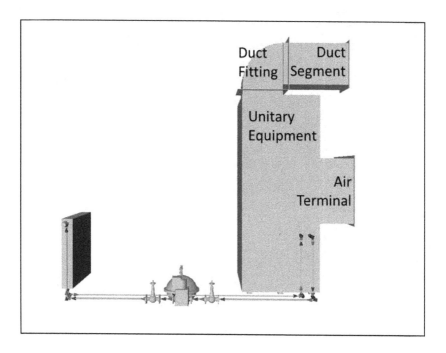

Figure 102: Bottom view of HeatPumpRadiator

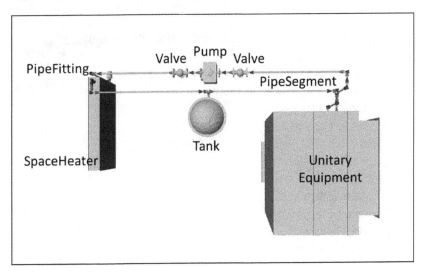

Properties have been specified via 568 relations. The radiator's components, like ducts, pipes and pump, have 90 ports. 45 relations describe connections of ports. Usually an out-port (source) connects to an in-port (sink) to enable a flow. A port connections expresses a functional, not a spatial connection, although the ports may touch in space.

Figure 103: Example assignment of a port

```
<ifc:IfcRelConnectsPortToElement GlobalId="..."Name="..." Descrip-
tion="Flow">
<ifc:RelatingPort xsi:type="ifc:IfcDistributionPort"... ref="i151" />
 <ifc:RelatedElement xsi:type="ifc:IfcUnitaryEquipment" ... ref="i53" />
</ifc:IfcRelConnectsPortToElement>
```

Figure 104: Example definition of an out-port

```
<ifc:IfcDistributionPort id="i151" GlobalId="..." Name="OutPort_915238" De-
scription="Flow" FlowDirection="source">
<ifc:ObjectPlacement xsi:type="ifc:IfcLocalPlacement" id="i299">
<ifc:PlacementRelTo xsi:type="ifc:IfcLocalPlacement" ... ref="i54" />
  <ifc:RelativePlacement>
   <ifc:IfcAxis2Placement3D>
    <ifc:Location Coordinates="-25.3999999999877 101. ..." />
    <ifc:Axis DirectionRatios="-1 0 0" />
    <ifc:RefDirection DirectionRatios="0 1 0" />
   </ifc:IfcAxis2Placement3D>
  </ifc:RelativePlacement>
 </ifc:ObjectPlacement>
</ifc:IfcDistributionPort>
```

Figure 103 shows the assignment of port i151 to the UnitaryEquipment i53, a 23 KW heat pump. Figure 104 essentially describes the port's placement.

Figure 105 states four systems IfcSystem and four relations IfcRelAssignsToGroup to form groups – one group per system. Three aggregations say that the space of interest on the ground floor belongs to a building and to a site. IfcRelContainedInSpatialStructure lists all entities of the site.

Figure 105: Concepts of HeatPumpRadiator model

Entity	Amount
IfcDuctSegment	3
IfcPipeFitting	12
IfcPipeSegment	18
IfcProject	1
IfcPump	1
IfcSite	1
IfcSpaceHeater	1
IfcSystem	4
IfcTank	1
IfcUnitaryEquipment	1
IfcValve	3
Relations	**729**
IfcRelAggregates	3
IfcRelAssignsToGroup	4
IfcRelAssociatesMaterial	1
IfcRelConnectsPorts	45
IfcRelConnectsPortToElement	90
IfcRelContainedInSpatialStructure	1
IfcRelDefinesByProperties	568
IfcRelDefinesByType	13
IfcRelServicesBuildings	4
EntityTypes	**10**
IFCAIRTERMINALTYPE	2
IFCDUCTFITTINGTYPE	1
IFCDUCTSEGMENTTYPE	1
IFCPIPEFITTINGTYPE	2
IFCPIPESEGMENTTYPE	1
IFCPUMPTYPF	1
IFCSPACEHEATERTYPE	1
IFCTANKTYPE	1
IFCUNITARYEQUIPMENTTYPE	1
IFCVALVETYPE	2

Figure 106: Pipe segments of the HeatPumpRadiator

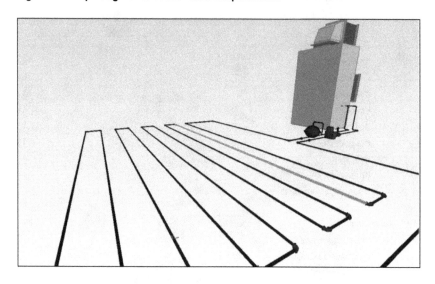

Figure 107: Waterpump of the HeatPumpRadiator

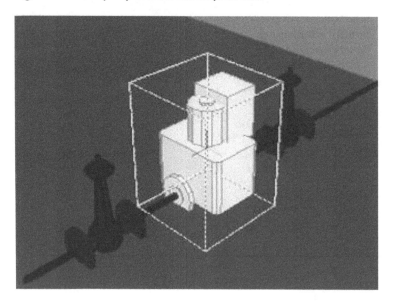

Model of a system

The HeatPumpRadiator is not modeled as one system with subsystems. The four systems of Figure 105 exist independently - the UnitaryEquipment, however, being a member of all systems.

We are going to consider System i123, named H_Vorlauf (HydronicSupply) and depicted in Figure 108.

Other systems define the hydronic return (H_Rücklauf) and the duct systems for air exhaust and air supply. They are distribution systems for air or water.

Figure 109 shows a group of diverse things – pump as well as ports and the UnitaryEquipment – the ingredients of system i123.

Figure 108: System *HydronicSupply*

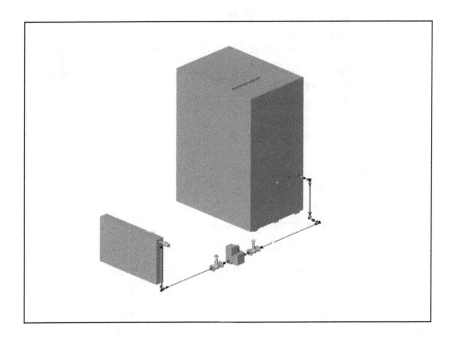

Figure 109: Definition of a group

```
<ifc:IfcRelAssignsToGroup GlobalId="...">
<ifc:RelatedObjects>
 <ifc:IfcPipeSegment ... ref="i7" />
 <ifc:IfcValve ... ref="i10" />
 <ifc:IfcPump ... ref="i13" />
 <ifc:IfcPipeSegment ... ref="i16" />
 <ifc:IfcValve ... ref="i18" />
 <ifc:IfcPipeSegment ... ref="i20" />
 <ifc:IfcSpaceHeater ... ref="i41" />
 <ifc:IfcValve ... ref="i44" />
 <ifc:IfcPipeSegment ... ref="i47" />
 <ifc:IfcPipeSegment ... ref="i49" />
 <ifc:IfcPipeFitting ... ref="i51" />
 <ifc:IfcUnitaryEquipment ... ref="i53" />
 <ifc:IfcPipeSegment ... ref="i56" />
 <ifc:IfcPipeSegment ... ref="i58" />
 <ifc:IfcPipeSegment ... ref="i60" />
 <ifc:IfcPipeFitting ... ref="i62" />
 <ifc:IfcPipeFitting ... ref="i64" />
 <ifc:IfcPipeFitting ... ref="i88" />
 <ifc:IfcDistributionPort ... ref="i128" />

     ... [List of 33 distribution ports] ...

</ifc:RelatedObjects>
<ifc:RelatingGroup ... ref="i123" />
</ifc:IfcRelAssignsToGroup>
```

Figure 110 presents the concept describing System i123, leaving away much syntactic detail. In essence the system is named, characterized by properties, and typed as a kind pipe segment made of pipes of copper (Kupfer) which are hard-soldered (Hartgelötet). The system remains un-structured and un-related, although it could be structured, like any object.

Figure 110: Excerpt of the concepts of System i123

```
<ifc:IfcSystem
    <ifc:IfcPipeSegmentType id="i122"
        Name="Pipe Types:Kupfer - Hartgelötet" ...
        PredefinedType="notdefined"></ifc:IfcPipeSegmentType>

    id="i123" Name="H_Vorlauf 2" ObjectType="H_Vorlauf">

<ifc:IfcPropertySet Name="Mechanical">
    Name="Number of Elements" 2
    Name="System Equipment" none
    Name="System Name" H_Vorlauf 2
    Name="Volume" 0.0003002226866766482
<ifc:IfcPropertySet Name="Mechanical - Flow">
    VolumetricFlowRateMeasure 0.00114
<ifc:IfcPropertySet Name="Other">
    Name="Category" Piping Systems
    Name="Family" Piping System: H_Vorlauf
    Name="Family and Type" Piping System: H_Vorlauf
    Name="Type" Piping System: H_Vorlauf
    Name="Type Id" Piping System: H_Vorlauf
</ifc:IfcSystem>
```

Figure 110 presents a terse description, saying little about configuration, function and operation, except for the properties Volume and Flow. The description carries information in form of properties, ports and port-connections.

Figure 111 explains one component, the UnitaryEquipment, in terms of its properties, placement and representation. Note the property-item *System Name*, a mechanical property. It lists the names of those systems UnitaryEquipment, belongs to, because it is a group-member. We would consider *System Name* a structural characteristic.

Other functional knowledge can be built into algorithms which simulate and evaluate the HeatPumpRadiator's proper functioning and performance must use background knowledge about the device's to determine performance. It will be function-related flows, forces, resources, processes, etc. R. Wimmer [Wimmer (2017)] explains how an IFC model serves energy performance simulation.

Figure 111: Description of UnitaryEquipment

```
<IfcUnitaryEquipment id="i53" Name="Heat Pump:23 kW:915238"
    ObjectType="23 kW"..................................................................
<IfcPropertySet Name="Pset_ElectricalDeviceCommon">
    Name="NumberOfPoles" 3
<IfcPropertySet Name="Constraints">
IfcPropertySet Name="Dimensions">
    Name="Area"> AreaMeasure 4.08484849285632
    Name="Volume"> VolumeMeasure 1.39908484437479
<IfcPropertySet Name="Electrical - Loads">
<ifc:IfcPropertySet Name="Identity Data">
<IfcPropertySet Name="Mechanical">
    Name="Drain Flow"> VolumetricFlowRateMeasure 0
    Name="External Static Pressure" PressureMeasure 248.84
    Name="System Classification" Sanitary, Power,
        Hydronic Return, Hydronic Supply, Return Air, Supply Air
    Name="System Name" H_Rücklauf 3, H_Vorlauf 2, Mechanical Abluft 2, Me-
    chanical Zuluft 1
    Name="Water Flow" VolumetricFlowRateMeasure 0.00114
    Name="Water Pressure Drop"PressureMeasure 59294.91
<IfcPropertySet Name="Mechanical - Flow">
    Name="Air Flow"> VolumetricFlowRateMeasure 1.22706
<IfcPropertySet Name="Other">
    Name="Type" Heat Pump: 23 kW............................................
<ifc:ObjectPlacement xsi:type="ifc:IfcLocalPlacement" id="i54">
<ifc:RefDirection DirectionRatios="0 1 0" />.................................
<ifc:Representation xsi:type="ifc:IfcProductDefinitionShape">

    ... [representational detail] ...    </ifc:IfcUnitaryEquipment>
```

This completes the system overview, having skipped many properties which would be relevant for simulating operation and performance.

The IFC schema architecture

Version 4 of the IFC schema was released in 2013. This schema's architecture dates back [Liebig (1999)] however. Figure 62 introduces layers of concepts to organize the myriad of concepts of the vast BIM domain.

The bottom layer contains most basic conceptual building blocks – the atoms to build molecules. The layer serves as an example in case because it represents the geometric entities needed to describe the shape and form of what e.g. figure 99 presents. In fact, a major part of the file used to generate this figure elaborates the geometry of things.

GeometryResourc builds on the standard ISO/CD 10303-42:1992 - Part 42 for Geometric and Topological Representation – the kind of things also captured by the Boundary ontology mentioned before. [GeometryResource (2017)] describes the concept.

The architecture's top layer contains domain specific concepts. They define, for instance, the components of the HeatPumpRadiator which belong to the HVAC domain. Since the BIM approach caters to several domains, it is more domain specific than the PLM approach we are going to sketch.

Concepts of the Core help implement what T. Liebich, a schema architect, calls Architecture Principles: concepts to achieve a modular structure of models, a means to share information between different disciplines of the AEC industry and a way to reuse model components.

The Core layer defines the most abstract concepts which will be specialized by the higher levels and should provide a stable base, untouched by future versions of the schema. This layer decomposes into two levels of abstraction:

- the Kernel
- the Core Extensions

The Kernel defines objects, relationships, type definitions, attributes and roles. Liebich considers it a meta model and a platform for model extensions. Kernel concepts (classes) can only reference resources.

Core Extensions refine concepts of the Kernel. For instance refinement of *IfcObject* yields *IfcProduct* and *IfcProcess*, *IfcDocument* etc. The Core layer, finally, helps define the interoperability layer on top of it. The latter defines Common concepts shared by domain and application models. They enable applications of the top-level Domain layer to plug into the Core – sometimes by using an adapter.

Frankly, we had never thought of an architecture of concepts for the network domain, but if we had, then Basic concepts would have built a kind of Core layer and concepts representing network elements like boards and nodes and proxys the domain layer. We had no need for interoperability among diverse domains. But we had been well advised to build a kind of Resource layer although we did not deal with the geometry of network elements. And the IFCschema architecture had been a welcome guide had we not worked on a DTD but on a schema. Schema technology, however, came too late for us. W3C published a specification in 2001 and a recommendation in 2012.

11

Sketch of a PLM Schema

The IFC schema is not the only choice to present the concepts of an industrial domain. The manufacturing industry had started years before the construction industry turning its attention to product lifecycle management (PLM) in order to achieve interoperability of tools, applications and business processes. For instance, one wants to input product model drafts to simulation software in order to find the optimum design (see Figure 118).

Many proprietary data formats have evolved in the vital domain as well as the schema we will briefly sketch. The PLM XML schemas of Figure 112 can be accessed at [PLM XML (2017)]. They are not standardized but promoted by a group of tool makers. The schemas Routelist, Classification, UGS, scheduling, MPM, Motion, FDS and Delta are minor schemas complementing the main schema. Merely the MRO schema relates to a specific industry, containing concepts such as *Aircraft*, *Crew*, *Fleet*, *FaultCode*, *PhysicalAircraftRevision* and *ServiceBulletin*. The Main schema is neutral with respect to any specific domain of application.

Figure 112: List of PLM schemas

Schema	Comment
PLM XML schema	Main schema
Annotation schema	
Constraint schema	
Delta schema	Change description
FDS schema	Feature Description
Mechatronics schema	
Motion schema	
MPM schema	Project management
MRO schema	Maintenance, Repair, Operations
PDM schema	Product Data Management
Scheduling schema	Internal representation
UGS schema	Wires, cables, connections
Business schema	
Classification schema	
RouteList schema	

The XML schemas for PLM and BIM vary considerably, both on formal grounds – how they use types, elements and attributes – and on ontological grounds. A concept named *Object* does not occur in the PLM schema and important concepts like *Structure* are custom-made.

We will neither present the PLM schema nor examples in any detail. Figures 114 to 117 must suffice to convey PLM concepts. Figure 114 presents a random sample of the ca. 600 concepts of the Main schema. With the exception of *Budget*, they hint at the topics of presentation and representation to be covered. Figure 115 shows the embedding of the PLM-concept *Product which has little in common with IfcProduct*. It inherits attributes and properties from concepts dubbed *Base* and passes them on to a handful kinds of product. Figure 115 also shows the concept *Instance* used primarily to describe structure. Figure 116 lists the relations of the schema and Figure 117, finally, shows a selection of inherited attributes – sometimes called meta-information.

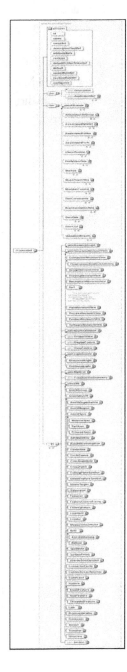

An elaborate concept – roughly sketched by the figure on the left – is used to define a product including its structure.

Structure definition in general comprises many diverse concepts and views: *Representations, DisplayControls, ViewControls, ProductViews, Materials, ConstructionGeometry, StructureRevisionViews, Sections* and *InstanceGraphs*. Structure may also specify part-connections, master structures and alternatives, variants and versions. Numerous concepts apply to describe product structure, for instance: *Root* means the top of a tree of InstancePaths.

InstancePath represents a path of InstanceThreads, top to bottom. The last InstanceThread relies on its 'ancestor' elements to define the path. Path children are formed by adding one or more InstanceThreads on the end of the path.

InstanceThread collects together Instances which correspond across different revisions of a structure.

InstanceGraph is an element used as a container for elements which represent an assembly graph. There may be more than one root, and the roots may be Instances or StructureRevisionViews.

Connection is a structured object which represents a connection between a number of InstancePaths in an assembly. *FlowConnection* describes the flow of energy or information.

Occurrence specifies a usage of a Structure, StructureRevision, or StructureRevisionView in an Assembly.

Structure navigators implement a popular user interface to structure: a parts list in form of a tree structure. BIM- and PLM-tools use them alike and though all trees look similar, they differ in meaning.

Figure 113 shows the structure of a building modeled in IFC style. It states that the space 3R01 contains two fans and is itself contained in a building storey named Roof which is contained in a building. Here, composition implies spatial containment which serves as a prime structuring principle of the IFC models. Decomposition expressed via relations occurs rarely as the clinic example shows.

Figure 113: Containment structure of a building

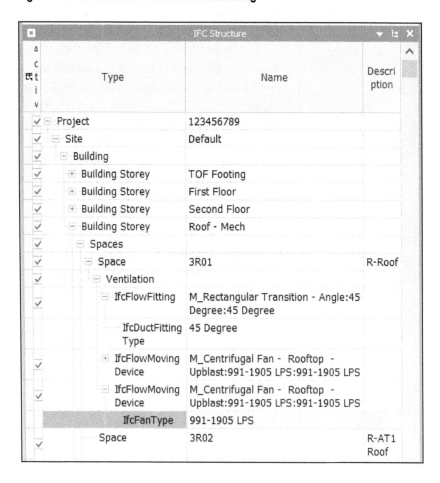

Composition differs in the PLM domain. Here, the notion prevails that any product or system is an assembly composed of sub-assemblies and parts. Such composition need not imply containment. It rather means, for instance, that precisely positioned mechanical parts connect, touch each other, are fixed by form or force and may rotate or translate within given constraints. Aggregation in the PLM domain, thus, is geared to express function rather than containment.

The schemas of PLM and IFC differ although both rely on objects (things), properties, relations and shape to capture domain content.

Models differ as well. BIM models may not have the complexity of PLM models, but usually comprise a great many more components. Still, models are compatible to some extent. IFC models have been transformed and imported into PLM CAD tools. PLM CAD designs have been exported conforming to IFC standards though with losses.

What makes models – diverse as their underlying schemas are – compatible? Has a conceptual core been found for modeling artifacts?

ISO 10303 – the fundamental and comprehensive Standard for the Exchange of Product Model Data (STEP) – did prepare common ground [ISO Standard 10303 (2017)]. Beginning at the turn of the millennium it defined, for instance, the Resources *Geometric Model* and *Product Structure Model* which influenced developments in PLM and BIM.

Conceptually, ISO standardization did not start from scratch. The engineering disciplines were well advanced and some engineering industries co-operated by sharing experience. Still, the standard had to create its own conceptual universe making strong ontological commitments to the views and concepts it standardized.

We consider this standardization effort a major challenge and achievement. After all, products had already reached enormous complexity and were of boundless variety. Anderl [Anderl (2000)] introduces to the development, implementation and industrial use of STEP.

Figure 114: Random selection of PLM concepts

Element	Complex type	Simple type
AbsoluteOccurrence	AbsoluteOccurrenceType	AccessIntentEnum
AccessControl	AccessControlBase	AlphaType
AccessIntent	AccessIntentType	anyURIType
Address	AddressType	AttenuationType
And	AndType	AttributeClassType
AssociatedAttachment	ApplicationRefType	AttributeOwnerType
AssociatedDataSet	ApplicationType	AxisFieldType
AttribOwner	AreaType	BooleanListType
Attribute	AssociatedAttachmtType	BoundingType
AttributeClass	AssociatedDataSetType	CompoundRepTypeEnum
AttributeContext	AttribOwnerBase	CoordinateFieldType
AttributeLegalOwner	AttributeBase	CoordinateSystemStyle
AttributeRef	AttributeClassBase	CurrencyType
Bound	AttributeContextType	CutoffAngleType
BSplineCurve	AttributeLegalOwnerType	DescriptionType
BSplineSurface	AttributeRefType	DirectionFieldType
Budget	BoundType	DirectionType
BudgetDefinition	BoxBoundType	DoubleListType
AbsoluteOccurrence	BSplineCurveType	DrawingStyleType

Figure 115 shows the inheritance structure of two important concepts *Product* and *Instance*. Managed Base is one of the abstract base classes which inherit attributes. It is used for elements which require information management such as access control, status and checkout information.

Figure 117 shows some attributes *Product* may have inherited. And properties may have been assigned like these:

JointAccelerationLimit, JointVelocityLimit, LengthProperty, MassProperty, MaterialSpecification, MaterialThickness, ModulusOfElasticity, OutsideDiameter, PoissonsRatio, RatedCurrent, RatedPower, RatedVoltage, SpecificHeatCapacity.

Figure 115: Context of the concepts Product and Instance

```
Id Base
    Description Base
        AttributeOwner Base
            Properties Base
                Managed Base
                    Structure Base
                        ProductType
                        Product
                            HarnessProduct
                            MROProduct
                            Aircraft
                        ProzessorProduct
                        RealizedProduct
                            PhysicalAircraft
```

```
Id Base
    Description Base
        AttributeOwner Base
            Properties Base
                ManagedBase
                    StructureUsageBase
                        InstanceBase
                        Instance
                            CompositionInstance
                            ConnectionInstance
                            FeatureInstance
                            SensorInstance
                            MechanismInstance
                            ProcessInstance
                            ProductInstance
                            SoftwareInstance
                            WorkareaInstance
```

Figure 116: Overview of relations

ManagedBase	PathElementRelation
GeneralRelation	PendingEventRelation
Allocation	PhysicalLogEntriesRelation
AllowedDeviationRelation	RealisedFromRelation
CharacteristicValueForRealisedProduc-tRelation	RemovedInstalledDesignProduc-tRelation
DefinitionRelation	RemovedInstalledPhysicalProduc-tRelation
DerivedFromRelation	
DiscrepancyPhysicalProductRelation	RemovedInstalledProductRelation
DiscrepancyProductRelation	RepresentedByRelation
DispositionApplicabilityRelation	RequestedLotRelation
ElementEventRelation	RequestedRealisedProductRelation
HasSubActivitiesRelation	ResourceAssignment
LocationAssignment	RouteNodeAssignment
LogEntryValuesRelation	RouteSectionAssignment
MROLocationRelation	ScheduleTaskDependency
MROSpecificationRelation	TraceabilityRelation
NeutralCharacteristicRelation	VendorPartRelation
PartApplicabilityRelation ...	

These relations add facets to the elaborate *Structure* concept which has evolved in the PLM domain. This concept intrigues us since it integrates a wide spectrum of views derived from experience. Whether it is the best concept conceivable we cannot claim, but it serves as a most valuable model.

Figure 117: Selection of attributes

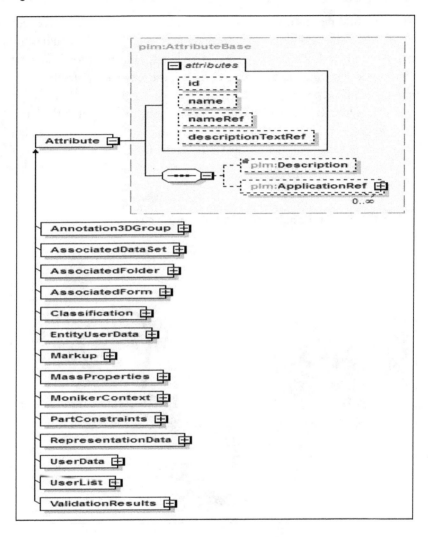

Model-based simulation

PLM und BIM models have yet to pass a special test. Product designers need to know whether a new creation functions, is possibly flawed or could be realized with less effort. The designer of a building wants to prove it does not squander energy and meets requirements. He may do that by simulating its operation and behavior.

The computer-simulations of a crashing car or the descent of the Lunar lander became famous. Such models can be mathematically demanding, they also need to know about the product – its precise form function and material.

In Figure 118 color visualizes the computed stress of the sprocket touching and driving a gear wheel.

Figure 118: Product design used for stress simulation

Modelica is a popular tool to build and run simulation models [Modelica 2018]. Its many libraries support model creation, offering predefined objects, connections and behaviors in domains such as *power systems, biochemical reactions, AC circuits, electromechanical drives and drive control*. Fundamental libraries are dedicated to electrical and mechanical phenomena and others.

The library AixLib supports Building Energy Performance Simulation (BEPS) [Pinheiro (2018)]. It contains packages to model Airflow, Boundary Conditions, Controls, Fluids, Media and Utilities.

Not all information contained in the IFC model of a building is relevant for BEPS, but much of it, in particular information on space (see Figure 95) and HVAC Systems (see Figure 101), also material properties, internal loads (stemming from people, lighting, etc.) and thermal zones. To construct a simulation model relevant information must first be filtered from a comprehensive IFC Model. A sophisticated IFC tool achieve the filtering – the Model View Definition (MVD) tool. Wimmer describes how the IFC schema is used to construct a filter (MVD) which extracts the needed information automatically [Wimmer (2017)]. Manual extraction of spatial information would be cumbersome and error prone.

Then a way must be found to map the filtered IFC objects, relations and properties onto the descriptive elements defined by AixLib. IFC properties must map onto the parameters and connections onto the equations used for simulation. This mapping process can be challenging for numerous reasons caused by limitations of the IFC model, such as missing IFC objects and properties. Detailed HVAC simulation models include pipes, ducts, valves (including heat and pressure losses), control schemes and energy consumption estimates.

Pinheiro fixed information deficits via work-arounds. Interestingly, he did he did not report any fundamental issues in deriving the simulation model from the IFC model [Pinheiro (2018)]. He values the flexibility of the IFC schema, which can be extended. And he argues that IFC models be of high quality – they should be thoroughly checked by rules. The only deplores that IFC models do not contain requirements. After all, simulation should demonstrate that a design meets demands.

The following example is taken from a research project [EBC Annex60 (2017)]. Figure 119 depicts three thermal zones of an office building. The rooms should have an air temperature of 21°C. People are present between 7:00 and

17:30. Their metabolic rate is that of a sitting person, emitting 80 Watt per square meter skin surface. Light switches on at 17:00. Computers and screens are active when people are present.

Because the offices are heading in different directions the operations of the zones to guarantee the thermal comfort is different. One side of the building is heading west and the other side east. The differences in the solar radiation require different heating. The corridor should have an air temperature of at least 15°C and the light be turned on at 16:30. Figure 119 shows the thermal zones in different colors.

Figure 119: Thermal zones in office space

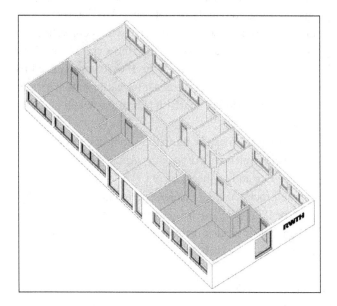

Figure120 shows a Modelica model for simulating the energy performance of the office building, using the AixLib library. It received input from an IFC model. Six thermal zones of the building and the heating system are presented. Many characteristics are modeled among them pump performance (9068 Pa) and volume flow (2.22 l/s).

Figure 120: *Thermal simulation model using AixLib.*

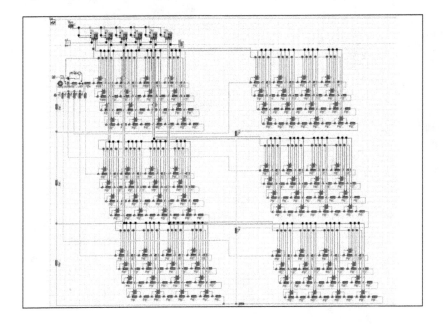

Part 3: Modern Models

12

Reflections on Modelling

Computers change the game

Having read about IFC's approach, readers may think it eclipses our early approach. Indeed, IFC took a different road and came a long way: it created a highly domain specific language – including many hundreds of objects and properties – some of which we have sketched. Computer-based tools master this language perfectly and who undertakes a design job on a computer receives immediate feedback: the current design in form of a sophisticated visual presentation one can check for flaws.

Language designers made several skilled moves. They separated a closed part of concepts, the IFC-schema, from an open part which lets the many players in the field contribute descriptions of new products and processes. See a user defined version of *IfcUnitaryEquiment* to model a heat pump including all properties needed to simulate its energy performance [Pinheiro (2018)]. *IfcBuildingElementProxy* also serves to extend the schema – at least for a closed group of users.

Language designers used a powerful means of representation, the XML schema, a standard and a suite of tools around it. They also relied on inheritance to achieve an efficient form of representation. It is defined both implicitly within the schema and explicitly via relations like *RelDefinesByType* as shown in the examples.

Our means had been much more modest. Besides DTDs, we experimented with the KRS Concept System [Steels (1986)]. This tool intrigued us since it implemented inheritance between concepts powerfully and elegantly.

Modern tools change the modeling practice of old: the models CAD tools yield are flawless and many-faceted. In our days, humans had to do the modeling with the help of drawing tools and text editors – an error-prone endeavor.

Therefore, we were concerned that ontological flaws would ruin a model. What if a computation process sports the characteristics *weight* and *color* which are unheard of. Such ontological nonsense may happen simply by allowing a system to inherit any kind of characteristic. Without views, we worried it would be next to impossible to assure a model's ontological consistency. Explicit views would make it feasible to detect and warn of a blue calculation.

Such worries matter less today since modern tools have the power to detect many kinds of implausibility. Rules can check the proper use of concepts in a model and much more. The research project STREAMER explores rules to check whether a building's design meets requirements or complies with national regulations [STREAMER (2017)]. Modern tools, thus, have changed the modeling game altogether.

Far sighted customers had envisaged these modern times. They had objected to our approach, using this argument:

> *Handbooks and DTDs will go out of fashion. We want computers to help us design and configure our network, perform checks and simulate performance. And what is more: we want to exchange such information since we must cooperate with our business partners more closely.*
>
> *Though you disseminate information concerning operation and maintenance successfully, if you would feed the knowledge of networks into a diagnostic-system, service could become a lot cheaper and we would do better. Eventually, we want to deploy foreign communication gear, since IP technology is catching on and we will have to operate open hybrid networks. This will challenge us.*

Our critics were right: in the long run, customers needed advanced tools. They even hoped for powerful knowledge-based tools which not only know about a network's bare technical facts but also capture everyday operational experience – rendering tools smart enough to take over routine parts of network operation.

Our critics sensed the great value a sophisticated network model would hold. And they would have welcomed today's achievements – the tools for network management, CAD, Enterprise Resource Planning (ERP), Product Data Management (PDM). And they would have taken interest in attempts to convert a model from XML to OWL, input it to an OWL reasoner, use it as a knowledge base and expand its scope.

To conceive a new domain

When we once considered turning dozens of Html-handbooks on network operation and maintenance into a knowledgebase to assist technicians, we were awed by the size, complexity and risk of the task since no guide existed we could follow.

Today, the scene has changed. Tools exist and much conceptual material has been compiled for numerous domains. One can become inspired by libraries of industry and cross-industry schemas [XML-Schemas (2016)], ontologies [Protegewiki (2017)] or by conceptual modeling languages [Verdonck (2016)].

National standardization bodies as well as international consortia define concepts. For instance, The Open Group pursues standards and conceptual models for the business domain creating The Open Group Architecture Framework [TOGAF 9.1 (2017)].

IFC's Resource layer as well as various IFC Kernel layer concepts mark a valuable resource. PLM represents valuable concepts, too, e.g. *Structure*.

In spite of this rich pool of concepts, the issue remains: *how to conceive a new domain*? Domains may differ substantially. The domains of business organizations and communication networks seem to have less in common than the BIM and PLM domains. How to determine a foreign domain's idiosyncrasies, views, functions and structures?

If we were to conceive a new domain, we would begin by studying common practice – the routines of work and ways of communication. We would identify popular and significant concepts and generalize them, then. scrutinize them for categories and points of view: will physical aspects play a major role or aesthetics or others? Once the domain revealed its nature we would design an architecture similar to IFC's conceptual architecture in Figure 62. The architecture must cater to the fact that concepts are composed of concepts and many concepts are like the components of a platform to be used throughout all modeling tasks. The architecture determines our ontological commitment – the commitment to what exists in the domain.

The rules of best practice of schema design would concern us too. After all, a complex schema should be understandable, usable, non-redundant, extensible and the resulting models fit for information processing.

At first sight, it seems simple to determine a conceptual base: all one needs are objects which have an identifier and a few metadata, as many properties as needed and possibly relations to other objects.

But how to proceed from there? Why define a concept like *IfcProduct* and how to determine its mandatory and optional features in order to suit a domain's many diverse products? Similar questions apply to Ifc*Process* and other core concepts.

Note the difference of *IfcProduct* and *IfcProcess*. A product has placement and representation in space which a process has not. *IfcProduct*, thus, guides modelers to specify some essentials of a building's static ingredients. *IfcProcess*, in contrast, does not lead modelers to capture the dynamic essence of a process: neither its start, end and steps in between, nor the flows involved, input, output, resources consumed, etc.

Of course, *IfcProcess* can be refined in many ways and in great detail. It may carry any number of properties and relate to any number of actors, resources, controls, products and other processes. All in all, *Ifc-Process* provides a terse and flexible descriptive scheme.

Yet, is this the way to go? How to define the core of concepts? Should the concept *System* be among them? We believe that the core's design must meet the practical challenges of representation – to model boundaries and bodies, function and structure, and keep complexity at bay.

About systems

We conceived a system-concept early on, assuming it would deal naturally with complex artifacts. After we had sketched the concept as in Figure 54, we considered it to be complete in an ontological sense since it covered all generic views we deemed relevant. And its Basic Concepts would define the conceptual core on which we could build.

Therefore, we expected IFC, PLM and other domains to have come forward with powerful system concepts, but were surprised that this was not the case. The PLM schemas, to the best of our knowledge, do not define a comprehensive system-concept. The aggregation-concept seems to suffice.

The Open Group Architecture Framework uses prose to describe the system features of *BuildingBlock* which:

- represents a (potentially re-usable) component of business, IT, or architectural capability that can be combined with other building blocks to deliver architectures and solutions.
- is a package of functionality defined to meet the business needs across an organization
- has a type that corresponds to the TOGAF content metamodel (such as actor, business service, application, or data entity)
- has a defined boundary and is generally recognizable as "a thing" by domain experts
- may interoperate with other, inter-dependent, building blocks
- considers implementation and usage and evolves to exploit technology and standards
- may be assembled from other building blocks.

IfcSystem, finally, is an IfcObject which is essentially defined by a group of typed things, as the example of the HeatPumpRadiator shows.

We were astonished when we found out that *IfcSystem* was not used in the Clinic example although hundreds of functional systems and subsystems could have been specified. An argument, which we cannot verify, explains this phenomenon: it says that a clinic's technical infrastructures tend to be constructed by using special CAD-tools. Their proprietary data formats do not always convert well to the IFC format and, therefore, systems do not appear in the example. A handbook describes the intricacies of mappings between the elements, properties and boundaries of the IFC format and the proprietary data format of a HVAC design tool [Revit (2018)].

We were not surprised, however, to find researchers arguing to use system concepts in the following case depicted in Figure 118 [Häfele (2017)].

175

Figure 121: Functional units of a clinic

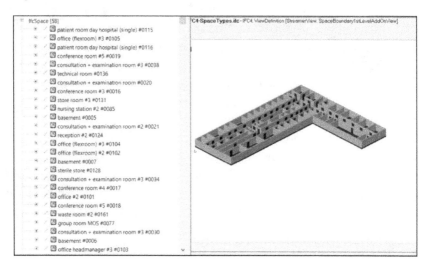

Figure 121 shows on the right the spatial structure of a clinic floor. On the left, all rooms are listed and carry a name: *Reception, Examination room, Nursing station, Office*, etc. The names refer to a function which remains undefined. In this context researchers argue for systems:

> *Each room should be modeled as a discrete functional system which is part of several super-systems for lighting, ventilation, etc. Since any sub-system consumes and exchanges energy and other resources, it should be assessed with respect to capacity and performance, criticality (how vital) and susceptibility to degradation or dysfunction. Moreover, the system view should be used throughout a room's life cycle, first to specify requirements, then to design various realizations and assess them.*

We also assume the room- systems can play a role in processes, e.g. the medical process (consultation, examination, treatment...) and the administrative process (reception ... discharge). So, there seem good reasons to eventually conceive a clinic as a comprehensive system with structure and function under various views.

Systems are being discussed among designers in the PLM domain, too. A tool maker expresses his vision like this:

176

Users should define, store and re-use cohesive sets of parts, features and constraints as a single functional system. Adjustable assemblies that allow adaptable placement and new motion analysis tools that automatically simulate mechanisms under the influence of forces reduce the need for physical prototypes.

At the heart of systems design are systems libraries, the capability to define, store and re-use complete systems of parts. More than just subassemblies, systems will retain the knowledge for re-use [SAG (2017)].

This argument lets us believe that a demand for expressive power exists which an advanced system-concept may fulfill. The System-concept can and should be developed further and refined to suit many domains.

About function

We struggled with the concept *Function* for some time. At first we considered *Function* a household word, until we pondered the function of an initial objects of interest: the ISDN network. Since *Function* seemed highly significant in this complex domain, we tried to define the view *SystemFunction* and integrate it with all the other system views we favored.

But none of our attempts worked out. *Function* ran counter to other views, was not categorical, not modular. It felt like an impurity until we realized that function and system is quite the same thing. A system implements a function and cannot be separated from its function. Eureka, the system-concept was all we needed.

Now it became obvious why we had struggled: any system feature can have functional significance. A function may address cause and effect, change, energies, forces, objectives, ports and flows, mechanisms and methods, time, form, and structure as well. Thus one will need many System-views to describe the many facets of function, including the technical and non-technical environments that embed a function. Figure 122 symbolizes this view.

177

Figure 122: Outline of the function-scheme

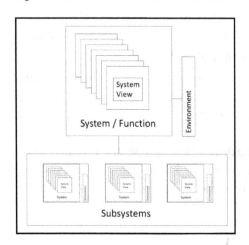

To describe a function is, of course, not only a matter of generic views – many scientific disciplines deal with function in a specific manner. Think of the functioning of a car's engine. If we are interested what happens in a combustion chamber when fuel is being injected, how piston and rod move and push, and whether they cause the crankshaft to self-oscillate. Here mathematics, simulation software, etc. come into play in order to define the engine's functional characteristics.

All in all, powerful means exist to model function. The clinic example lists more than a hundred thousand assignments of functional properties.

About structure

Modeling structure matters, because artifacts in all domains tend to be structured, often not only in one but in several ways. The many structures of boundaries and bodies tell the tale.

In the past we tried and also failed to devise ways of capturing structure. Today, we deem modeling structure to be the fine art of modeling. Spatial structure, shapes and forms, in particular, reached a high level of sophistication in several domains – BIM and PLM as well as Computer Generated Imagery CGI.

Boundaries other than physical surfaces may be less challenging – the structure of transition for instance. Composition may be intricate at times, order trivial, interaction – notably the interaction of systems – remaining a field of research on structure.

We found function and structure to be intertwined at times. When we functionally decompose an organization into departments, we imply the decomposition of its rights, duties and resources, and of the flows of funds and information, etc.

A medically inclined colleague once tackled the daunting task of modeling the anatomic structure and function of arm and shoulder – muscles and bones, ligaments and nerves, skin and vessels, the flow of signals, lymph, blood, nutrients and heat, also force and kinematics.

She learned a lot about structure which was the point of the exercise. And she inspired a musically inclined colleague to model the structure of transition of a Beethoven concert: themes and variations, counterpoints, keys and time, strings, winds etc.

Although such attempts remained mere exercises, we learned about the challenges, for instance the challenge of modeling the ways physical boundaries and bodies connect – the connectivity of elements.

If we were to conceive a new domain we would attempt to devise a structure-schema by drawing on the experiences made in the course of structuring clinics, devices, software and organizations. It should complement the Property-schema.

While pondering such issues, a little episode came to mind which happened in the past:

> We felt we made headway in conceiving structure when we turned our focus away from structure-in-general – sometimes just a list of relations – and turned to the structure of systems. When we decomposed a system into sub-systems and discriminated types of structure according to system-views, then our structures began to look well-formed. And they told more than the lore of parts and wholes.

About views

We used about a dozen views to construct concepts – views which we deemed to stand for the gist of the matter in our domain. Other domains favor other views. *3D-space* seems prominent in the domain of architecture. In the network domain, on the other hand, *3D-space* plays a marginal role since the shape and placement of communication nodes and radio links matter little.

Electronics and software play a dominant role and the logical view applies to most network components. In the network domain, *Product* would, thus, not carry built-in views of form and location. *Process*, in contrast, might carry the characteristics *Network-location* and *Form-of-change* – telling where and how a process changes the network.

The view *Change* does not seem prominent in the BIM domain. We assume that the construction process loses significance after it delivered its result, the building. And the myriad of changes caused by each of the very many steps of construction are perhaps not worth documenting. Buildings also change little with time even though tenants may come and go. Only the models of buildings change frequently in the course of the design process.

Communication networks, on the other hand, have been changing all the time by being extended, upgraded and reconfigured. This change matters since it may cause flaws and trigger action.

Apparently, every domain justifies its own modeling style, dominated by key views like space, information processing or change. They can be hard-wired to concepts as in the case of *IfcProduct* or, as in the case of Basic Concepts, be used as needed.

The term *View* is popular in all domains we have come across, but differs in meaning. The views of UML in Figure 43 stand for types of diagram.

The Open Group Architecture Framework speaks of an Architecture view, Business process domain view, Management, Engineering and Stakeholder view.

PLM uses ConnectionView, ProductStructureView, ConfigurationView and the views *Design* and *Production*.

IFC defines domain views like *HVAC* (Heating, Ventilating and Air Conditioning) by long lists of concept names – the things relevant to HVAC. IFC also uses Model View Definitions (MVD). A model view defines a model's content as required for a certain phase or milestone of construction, e.g. HVAC construction. IFC mentions numerous views: the Structural analysis view, Coordination view and Design transfer view and also speaks of 9 component models which present views. Among them are:

- **The Architectural model**, a model for design coordination, defines the spaces and the visual outlook of the building including the surfaces and used materials.

- **MEP model(s)** MEP stands for Mechanical, Electrical and Plumbing.
- **The Structural system model** defines the engineering level model of the building's structure.

No doubt, these views play an important role, because they help apply the strategy *Divide and Conquer* to break a problem or task down into manageable parts.

We have restricted views to concepts and systems. Others apply views to an entire domain. Such broadviews are not categorical and frequently overlap in scope. Still, most views, we assume, have proven their worth in practice.

About quality

The question *what is a quality concept* concerned us at the very start. Many concepts we considered to use felt like a bad choice: fuzzy, ill-defined and possibly complicated. Terms like function, risk, asset and maintenance gave us a headache: how to turn them into concepts a computer could use? Since we felt at risk we turned to certain views, discriminations and in due course concepts we deemed high quality, because they were clear cut. But this would solve only part of the quality issue, we guessed. As told in Part 2 we therefore considered many sides of the issue. We even pondered whether an algorithm could analyze models, DTDs and ontologies and identify concepts which are ill-designed or impractical. But to no avail.

An algorithm eventually analyzed the IFC schema producing various metrics such as statistics of inheritance [Amor (2015)]: ca. 10% of concepts, called root entities, do not inherit from concepts, all others do. The average Depth of the Inheritance Tree (DIT) is four levels of abstraction, the maximum eight. For an example see Figure 67. Such metrics tell us little about quality because, unfortunately, we still don't know how inheritance patterns affect, say, a schema's ease of use or a model's expressiveness.

Fortunately, schemas are used, tested and criticized as they evolve. The release of the schema IFC4 addressed some 1200 change requests [Amor (2015)]. Such strong feedback from the field reveals quality concerns better than any algorithm could.

Thus, one hardly needs to worry about the quality of schemas and tools for the BIM and PLM domains. After all, thousands of engineers are creating sophisticated models of complex artifacts which serve their purpose well.

Still, tool developers are pushing on, envisioning advanced schemas, various forms of model representation and toolkits which offer means of collaboration and integrate applications. And the Seminar *Automated Reasoning on Conceptual Schemas* considered intelligent design tools [Cavalese (2013)].

We are looking ahead with interest. But looking back also piques our curiosity: Do we understand the art of conceiving a domain and developing its schema? And are we prepared to pass this knowledge on? It would be the kind of expertise we were sorely missing, decades ago.

Epilogue, Abbreviations, References, List of Figures, About the Authors

Epilogue

We have benefitted from many teachers. We mention the following few, because we owe them essential insights when we entered new terrain. They directed our train of thought.

Thomas Aquinas provided the capstone to our selection of discriminations.

Aristotle's metaphysics introduced us to categorical points of view which simplified the conception of an endless variety of things.

John F. Sowa's seminal book *Conceptual Structures – Information Processing in Mind and Machine* explained the concept *Concept*.

Ludwig Wittgenstein's thinking on logic and language let us believe that an ontology is essentially about practical concepts, not formalisms, to master the world around us.

Abbreviations

AEC	Architecture, Engineering & Construction
BIM	Building Information Modeling
CA-	Computer Aided
CAD	Computer Aided Design
CAM	Computer Aided Manufacturing
ERM	Entity Relationship Model
IFC	1. Industry Foundation Classes
	2. the organizations promoting Industry Foundation Classes, notably buildingSMART International Ltd.
HVAC	Heating, Ventilating and Air Conditioning
MEP	Mechanical, Electrical, Plumbing
MVD	Model View Definition
PLM	Product Lifecycle Management
SGML	Standard Generalized Markup Language
TOGAF	The Open Group Architecture Framework
UML	Unified Modeling Language
XML	Extensible Markup Language

References

Amor, R. (2015) Analysis of the Evolving IFC Schema. In Proc. of the 32nd CIB W78 Conf., Eindhoven, The Netherlands

Anderl, R. et al. (Ed.) (2000) STEP STandard for the Exchange of Product Model Data. B.G. Teubner, Stuttgart

Andersen, O. et al. (2007) Building an Ontology of CAD Model Information. In Geometric Modelling, Numerical Simulation, and Optimization. ISBN 978-3-642-08831-5

Aristoteles (1970) Metaphysik. Reclam, Stuttgart

Borrmann, A. et al. (Ed.) (2015) Building Information Modeling – Technologische Grundlagen und industrielle Praxis. Springer Vieweg, ISBN 978-3-658-05606-3

bSI (2017) http://www.buildingsmart-tech.org/specifications/ifc-releases/ifc4-add2

Cavalese, D. et al (Ed.) (2013) Automated Reasoning on Conceptual Schemas. Dagstuhl Report, Dagstuhl Publishing, Germany

EBC Annex 60 (2017) BPS Code Generation from Building Information Models. http://www.iea-annex60.org/finalReport/activity_1_3.html

Grochla, E. (Ed.) (1980) Handwörterbuch der Organisation, Poeschel Verlag, Stuttgart

GeometryResource (2017) http://www.buildingsmart-tech.org/ifc/IFC2x3/TC1/html/ifcgeometryresource/ifcgeometryresource.htm

Häfele, K.-H. (2017) Private communication

ISO Standard 10303 (2017) https://en.wikipedia.org/wiki/ISO_10303

Liebich, T. (2009) IFC 2x3 Model Implementation Guide. buildingSMART International

Modelica (2017) https://www.modelica.org/

OWL (2017) http://www.w3.org/Submission/OWL-S/

Pinheiro, S. et al. (2017) MVD based information exchange between BIM and building energy performance simulation. Automation in Costruction 90 (2018) 91–103

PLM XML (2017) https://www.plm.automation.siemens.com/en/products/open/plmxml/schemas.shtml

Protegewiki (2017) https://protegewiki.stanford.edu/wiki/Protege_Ontology_Library#OWL_ontologies

Revit (2018) Revit IFC Handbuch. Revit GmbH, Munich

SAG (2017) Business communication on proprietary PLM modeling tools, Siemens AG

Shank, R. and Riesbeck, C. (1981) Inside Computer Understanding. Lawrence Erlbaum, Hillsdale

Sowa, J. F. (1984) Conceptual Structures – Information Processing in Mind and Machine. Addison Wesley, Reading

Steels, L. (1986) The KRS Concept System. Technical Report 86-1, AI Lab, Vrije Universiteit Brussel, Brussels

STREAMER (2017) http://www.streamer-project.eu/Downloads

sysML (2017) http://www.omg.org/spec/SysML/20150709/SysML.xmi

TOGAF 9.1 (2017) http://www.opengroup.org/subjectareas/enterprise/togaf/

Verdonck, M. and Gaily, F. (2016) Insights on the Use and Application of Ontology and Coneptual Modeling Languages in Ontology-Driven Concepual Modeling. In Comyn-Wattiau (Ed.) Conceptual Modeling, Proceedings 35th Intl. Conf., ER 2016, Springer, ISBN 978-3-319-46396-4

Wamsley, P. (2012) Definitive XML Schema, Prentice Hall, Ann Arbor

Wimmer, R. et al. (2017) Realizing openBIM – Development of a BIM Model View Definition for Advanced Building Energy Performance Simulation. Gebäudetechnik in Wissenschaft & Praxis,4, 276-291

Wimmer, K. and Wimmer N. (1992) Conceptual Modeling Based on Ontological Principles. Knowledge Acquisition, 4, 387-406

XML-Schemas (2017) http://www.xmlschema.info/xml_schema_library.html

Index of Figures

About the authors

Nancy Wimmer is an entrepreneur and an advisor to the World Council of Renewable Energy. She holds a Masters of Philosophy.
See her website at www.microsolar.com.

Klaus Wimmer, an engineer and IT specialist, served industry for many years. His doctoral thesis treats knowledge representation and modeling.

He also likes to write entertaining stories such as the book *A Bot under Gödel's Curse.*

We are interested in your opinion on the matter of the book.
Contact us at kw@microsolar.com

www.ingramcontent.com/pod-product-compliance
Lightning Source LLC
Chambersburg PA
CBHW071150050326

40689CB00011B/2059